Adrian Higgins

The Secret Gardens of Georgetown

BEHIND THE WALLS OF WASHINGTON'S MOST HISTORIC NEIGHBORHOOD

ADRIAN HIGGINS

PHOTOGRAPHS BY MICK HALES

LITTLE, BROWN AND COMPANY

BOSTON · NEW YORK · TORONTO · LONDON

First Edition

Library of Congress Cataloging-in-Publication Data

Higgins, Adrian.
    The secret gardens of Georgetown : behind the walls of Washington's most historic neighborhood / Adrian Higgins ; photographs by Mick Hales.
        p.   cm.
    ISBN 0-316-36084-8
    1. Gardens—Washington (D.C.)   2. Georgetown (Washington, D.C.)
    I. Title.
    SB466.U65W364 1994
    712´.6´09753—dc20   93-6334

Produced by Archetype Press, Inc., Washington, D.C.

Project Director: Diane Maddex
Art Director: Marc Alain Meadows
Assistant Art Director: Robert L. Wiser
Assistant Editor: Gretchen Smith Mui

Published simultaneously in Canada by
Little, Brown & Company (Canada) Limited

10 9 8 7 6 5 4 3 2 1
Printed in Italy

Opening photographs. Front jacket: Entrance to a Georgetown garden. Page 1: Spring flowers in bloom at the Bull residence. Pages 2–3: Houses lining the historic Chesapeake and Ohio Canal. Page 5: Dumbarton Oaks in autumn. Pages 6–7: Climbing roses at Dumbarton Oaks. Pages 8–9: Dogwood in the Foster garden. Page 10: A bench at Oak Hill Cemetery. Pages 12–13: "Georgetown and the Federal City, or the City of Washington," a colored engraving by T. Cartwright, from a drawing by George Beck, 1801 (Library of Congress). Pages 22–23: A row of Federal-era houses in spring. Pages 124–25: The rolling landscape of Oak Hill Cemetery. Pages 174–75: A view of Key Bridge and the Virginia shoreline from Washington Harbour. Page 240: Tools of the trade in the Krakora garden.

CONTENTS

Victorian Georgetown

A Modern Village

$\mathcal{A}$CKNOWLEDGMENTS

A large part of writing is assembling the knowledge of others. Many people lent me their time, patience, and expertise to create this book. Karen Fishler gave early encouragement and advice and pointed me to Diane Maddex, whose faith ran deep.

I am indebted to the professional expertise of landscape architects, designers, and horticulturists, among them Guy Williams, the late Lester Collins, James van Sweden, Wolfgang Oehme, Lila Fendrick, Yunghi Epstein, John G. Shaffer, Sarah Broley, Lucinda Friendly Murphy, Gordon Riggle, Philip S. Page at Dumbarton Oaks, and Stephanie Oberle at Tudor Place.

I also thank the professional gardeners, including Earl Loy at Pamela Harriman's garden, Peter Schenk, Richard Miller, and, in particular, Eddie Allen at Evermay and George Hunsaker at the Old Stone House, the last being the most valuable public servant in Washington. At Oak Hill Cemetery, Joseph and Ella Pozell helped me understand the beauty of their world.

For historical information and perspective, I learned much from the staff of the Smithsonian Institution and from Ronald M. Johnson, professor of history at Georgetown University. My biggest debt in this area, however, goes to Bob Lyle, curator of the Peabody Room at the Georgetown Regional Branch of the Washington, D.C., Public Library, whose encyclopedic knowledge of his village, its houses, and its people was valuable and uplifting.

It is always dangerous to quantify debt, but my deepest thanks must go to the owners of the gardens, who went beyond granting access and instead gave me a part of themselves. In many instances, their cooperation grew into friendship. I thank them all and especially Deedy Ogden, Harry Belin, Amie Block, Barbara Woodward, Polly Fritchey, James van Sweden, Oatsie Charles, Dick Bull, Joseph Krakora, Brewster and Stephany Knight, Susan Mary Alsop, Nan McEvoy, and Evelyn Nef.

I especially thank photographer Mick Hales for his expertise and sensitivity and for showing me Georgetown through fresh eyes. Similarly, Christine Simoneau offered advice and the clear-sighted observations of the artist.

Finally, without the support of my wife, Trish, this book simply would not have seen the light of day.

My friend Jane Brown, unwittingly, also was an early source of inspiration. Lecturing at The George Washington University, she reinforced my own view that Georgetown contains an unparalleled concentration of walled gardens. The book does not pretend to chronicle them all—space and time have robbed many worthy gardens of their glory—but I hope that in swinging open the gates to a few of them, I have shown that the spirit of gardening is alive and well in the nation's capital and that the American city is far from dead.

Although in most cases the gardens here are relatively new—given the short lives of many gardens and the long history of Georgetown—they are presented in the book according to the general age of their houses and sites themselves to provide a portrait of Georgetown's evolution. One exception is Dumbarton Oaks, a historic estate that is placed in the golden era of the 1920s, during which its gardens truly blossomed.

The Secret Gardens of Georgetown

INTRODUCTION

Outdoor spaces that flow from the house. Statues of animals and gods. Vine-covered arbors. Fountains, basins, and fish ponds. Plants grown for their ornament and fragrance. Murals and mosaics. These descriptions are not of the Georgetown garden but of ancient Rome. The same components—some widely altered, others remarkably not—are found today in Georgetown, not because its gardeners have tried to recreate Pompeii but because the need for a garden remains constant. People need plants, and people in cities need plants the most. A single rose can silence airplanes and cars. A cascading fountain banishes heat and dust. A camellia displaces the bustle and stress of life. The Romans knew that we must be in touch with nature, and Georgetowners still know this.

Visitors to Georgetown, Washington's most famous and historic neighborhood, recognize the gardening sentiment in the tended beds at the foot of street trees, the small front gardens, and the plants trained up walls and over arches. But the full bounty is hidden behind Georgetown's public face. Its private world contains a remarkable concentration of lovely gardens. One purpose of this book is to show how well this atavistic craving for plants has been satisfied in these inner sanctums.

Not too long ago, one of the Georgetowners whose garden is included in this book saw a need to clip the hedge at the bottom of her garden. As she tackled the chore, she was distracted by the presence of some people in an adjoining garden. Peeking over the fence, she saw the unmistakable faces of Bill Clinton and Al Gore. In any other neighborhood, such a vision might have been put down to hallucination. In Georgetown, it is par for the course.

Presidents have long wandered here, and it was George Washing-

ton's love of the place that influenced him to put the nation's capital where it is, on the other side of Rock Creek. Two haunting images of presidents and Georgetown persist: that of the gaunt, grieving Abraham Lincoln visiting his son's grave at Oak Hill Cemetery during the Civil War and that of John Kennedy dining at the home of newspaperman Joe Alsop in 1962. Normally vivacious and gossipy at such events, the president seemed preoccupied and engaged in animated discussion at the bottom of the garden with his designated ambassador to Moscow. "I was sitting by the president, and I knew him well enough to know that something was up," says Susan Mary Alsop. The next day news broke of the Cuban missile crisis.

What has all this to do with gardens? An account of Georgetown landscapes without their social, historical, and political context would be as hollow as a description of the eighteenth-century English landscape garden without noting the philosophies that drove it or of Versailles without mentioning the Sun King's view of his place in the universe a century earlier.

The fate of Georgetown's gardens has been entwined with the fortunes of the nation since the time George Washington and his city planner, Pierre Charles L'Enfant, arrived to map out the capital in 1791. Georgetown, named for George II, had been established in 1751, four decades earlier. As the closest port to the tobacco fields of Maryland and Virginia, the town had flourished under the guiding hand of its founders, Scottish merchants.

They built large, isolated country houses in the fields on the northern fringes of Georgetown, known as Georgetown Heights. Closer to the water, Federal-style rowhouses of more urban grace began to fill the gridded blocks. Designed by builders, not architects, they put unadorned comfort above architectural preening and took on the names of their early distinguished occupants, among them John Stoddert Haw, Susan Wheeler Decatur, and Henry Foxall. Houses also were named for later luminaries, including Alexander Graham Bell and Robert Todd Lincoln. As larger ships sailed and steamed to deeper ports, Georgetown's second industry—the new national government—took up the economic slack. Construction of the Chesapeake and Ohio Canal in the 1830s revived commercial Georgetown by linking the port to the coal fields of Appalachia. But it was never to be the industrial hub it once was: the railroads, which bypassed Georgetown, saw to that. Even so, by the 1850s Georgetown's first century had taken it from an agrarian colony to a bustling town. Creation of a "wilderness" at Georgetown's Oak Hill Cemetery, begun in 1849, indicated that by then there was a city to escape from.

After the Civil War Georgetown saw its fortunes diverge: large Victorian houses were built as status symbols while pockets of poverty emerged and festered. And in spite of an economic slump, the port's ignoble loss of its town council, and its full absorption into Washington in 1871, the period saw the largest spurt of house construction. Infill development of speculative rowhouses occurred until the early years of this century, principally to house civil servants. It was this secondary growth that today gives Georgetown–gentrified—its face as a quaint urban village. Amid the Federal rows, narrow brick townhouses were built while the once-rural district north of Q Street began to fill out.

By 1920 Georgetown had reached rock bottom. The waterfront was a center of shanties and noxious industry, and while a few old-guard Brahmins carried on Victorian social traditions, there was no collective sense of Georgetown's worth or history. This began to change when visionary new owners such as Robert and Mildred Bliss and Lammot and Frances Belin reclaimed Georgetown's lost country estates and the Colonial Revival movement took hold, fueled by the restoration of Williamsburg in the late 1920s.

Georgetown's ascendancy was assured, however, with the election of Franklin Roosevelt. His New Deal engendered a modern national government, and congressmen and government officials flocked to join the diplomats in Georgetown, initiating its slow but inevitable resurrection. Georgetown's fortunes got a further lift with the influx of political, civilian, and military officials during World War II and the ensuing Cold War, among them a thirty-year-old congressman from Boston named John Fitzgerald Kennedy. He lived in a total of seven Georgetown houses as a renter and owner before finding new lodgings on Pennsylvania Avenue. As Kennedy raised Georgetown's social currency, the historic preservation movement set about guiding the rebirth of its Federal and Victorian architecture and, by extension, the landscape architecture. For the first time owners turned their attention to the gardens. The wealthiest among them called on landscape architects such as Rose Greely and Perry Wheeler to recreate formal town gardens with southern and classical allusions. In 1950 Congress passed a law to protect Georgetown's historic buildings and gave the U.S. Commission of Fine Arts power to regulate renovations, additions, demolition, and new construction.

During this golden age Georgetown developed a reputation as a leader in historic preservation and the seat of America's governing liberal intelligentsia: in government, politics, foreign affairs, the law, and journalism. The latter stereotype holds to a degree, but Georgetown today is inhabited not by just one type, unless you count the cultivated. Nuns, students, financiers, artists, developers, the young, the old, families, and retirees all live in close quarters. The Fates have woven a rich human tapestry, which brings us to the book's second purpose.

At first blush the gardens featured here bear similarities as a result of prevailing landscape tastes and the shared fabric of red brick, walled spaces, and a regional plant palette. Closer examination, however, reveals the astonishing individuality of each garden and its owners and designers. No two are the same. This might be expected. But when one looks at these gardens collectively, the variety is remarkable and telling. Everyone, it seems, expresses his or her own love of nature differently.

Sentiment as much as good sense drove Georgetown's location. The colonial port linked tobacco growers to their markets, but its site also reminded Scottish founders of their beloved Dumbarton. Opening page: A ram's head relief calls up ancient Rome at the Krakora garden. Left, above: By 1830 Georgetown was a thriving port. Its Chesapeake and Ohio Canal, carried by a viaduct across the Potomac, connected the Atlantic seaboard with the Midwest. (Washingtoniana Division, D.C. Public Library) Left, below: Within two decades Georgetown had become the capital's favorite residential area. (Washingtoniana Division, D.C. Public Library)

*T*urn-of-the-century photographs chart Georgetown's evolution. Right, above: Georgetown University's spires still look down upon river traffic, but the steamships are long gone. (Washingtoniana Division, D.C. Public Library) Right, below: The house of Francis Scott Key, demolished for a ramp of the Whitehurst Freeway, was drawn into the shabby face of the late Victorian waterfront. (Washingtoniana Division, D.C. Public Library) Opposite: About 1890 the electric trolley furnished efficient transportation along streets now thick with traffic and pedestrians. (Robert A. Truax, Peabody Room, Georgetown Regional Branch Library)

But a common thread can be found: a shared appreciation of the garden and the common view that ownership of a beautiful garden is one of life's great uplifting experiences, akin to collecting fine art or rare books or playing in a string quartet.

And what does it tell us about the state of modern architecture and city planning that the most thriving urban village in Washington was laid out and built, for the most part, across the span of the nineteenth century? The passionate loyalty Georgetowners have for their community is no secret. The houses are loved because they are beautifully formed from beautiful materials by artisans. Most of all, everything is on a human scale.

While the houses for the most part are maintained with an eye toward historical accuracy, the gardens are not. It would not do to have outhouses and landfills and swine running back and forth. Today, these private outdoor spaces are too precious to waste on utility, and more care and love and money have been lavished on them than ever before. Like the gardens of far-off Roman citizens, they have been fashioned into private and personal visions of paradise.

First came building restoration and then the creation of delightful gardens. Opposite, above: The Charles residence now has a mansard roof and an even more spellbinding curtain of vegetation than in this 1870s view. (Peabody Room, Georgetown Regional Branch Library) Opposite, below: Today's Dumbarton Oaks is almost unrecognizable in its Victorian incarnation. (Historical Society of Washington, D.C.) Left: The Old Stone House began life as a place of commerce and ended that way, as a sign painter's shop and later a used-car dealership, before the federal government stepped in to preserve the oldest building in Washington. At the back of the house flowers now reign where cars once were parked. (Historical Society of Washington, D.C.)

The New
Republic

$\mathcal{T}$HE OLDEST SURVIVOR

If the role of a city garden is to transport visitors from the realm of noise, fumes, and concrete to a place of soothing tranquillity, few succeed as well as the Old Stone House garden. The passing pedestrian gets a hint of what is inside. In high summer there is a palpable drop in temperature, the city air is perfumed by the heady scent of an old rose, and, emotionally at least, one is drawn into a place of shade, color, beauty, fragrance, and mystery. For those enticed inside, the journey from modern clamor to earthly paradise is complete. From April to October visitors and Georgetowners alike find a garden whose three main herbaceous borders—two straddling a wide, sloping lawn—march on for more than a hundred feet to produce a magical balance of excitement and serenity. It is as if someone had taken the most vibrant heart of a grand English estate garden and placed it right in the thick of a bustling city.

Old shade and ornamental trees provide structure through the winter, but this is essentially a garden that hibernates during the dark side of the year. A *Cornus mas,* one of the oldest specimens in Washington, offers its golden yellow flowers in March as the daffodils bloom and nearly three thousand pastel-shaded tulips spring from the earth. April and May are the months of transition, when perennials emerge and creep over the bare black earth. Around Memorial Day the metamorphosis is complete. The 'Blush Noisette', 'Mme. Alfred Carrier', and 'Paul's Himalayan Musk' join the ranks of other heritage roses in their first and best show of sweetly fragrant flowers, the lemony buds of foxglove open a speckled purple, and larkspur provide a blue haze along the ground. This cycle is succeeded by another—bearded iris, herbaceous peonies, and about seventy strategically placed rugosa roses. In August, when most Washington gardens are frazzled and colorless, the Old Stone House garden is reborn with flowering crape myrtle, vitex, and masses of white-flowering phlox, rudbeckias, hollyhocks, lythrum, and, at last count, fifteen hundred 'Royal Standard' hostas.

The season winds down slowly as the garden captures that mellowest of times in the Washington garden—the month or so in early fall before the deciduous and herbaceous plants change color and recede. The repeat-blooming varieties of rose flower on, sporadically, while others decorate their spaces with orange-red hips. At the foot of the ancient crape myrtle at the midpoint of the west border, large flowering autumn crocuses, their white centers bleeding to lavender, poke through a sea of fresh, green-and-white striped ribbon grass interspersed with the nodding white and yellow flowers of Japanese anemone.

The story behind this happy place is really two stories: that of the Old Stone House itself and that of a quiet, gentle gardener named George Hunsaker.

Even in the context of Georgetown's rich building history, the Old Stone House stands out as an incongruously rustic structure on the modern city face of M Street. Built in 1766 by a cabinetmaker as a workshop and dwelling (a rear wing was added a decade later), the house is a rare surviving example of vernacular colonial architecture and the oldest surviving building in both Georgetown and the District of Columbia. The house was once touted as the place George Washington sat down to map out the federal city as well as the office of his planner, Pierre Charles L'Enfant, but this claim is not supportable. Its early pre-Revolutionary style and fabric of stone—reminiscent of Pennsylvania cottages of the period—set it apart from the red brick Federal houses that followed. During its life it passed through many hands and saw many uses, ending up in the 1950s as a used-car dealership and parking lot. Historic preservationists, then part of a nascent movement in Georgetown and the nation, persuaded Congress to buy the property in 1950. After a decade of restoration, it was opened by the National Park Service as a museum and today attracts thousands of tourists, schoolchildren, and other visitors each year.

*G*ardener George Hunsaker's
love affair with perennials keeps
the Old Stone House garden as
fresh in early autumn as in spring.
Opening page: Heavily scented
climbing roses provide the hook
for passers-by in May. Detail: In
September white-flowering
Japanese anemones play against
the dramatic markings of an old
crape myrtle. Opposite: The lawn
becomes a meadow for lunchtime
picnics. Left: The entrance terrace
welcomes visitors to the secret
refuge off busy M Street.

Original plans called for a formal, three-tiered Williamsburg-style colonial garden. A garden of colonial-era herbs was planted in the 1960s, but the grander scheme fortunately was abandoned, for it would have been as inauthentic as George Hunsaker's creation but with little of its charm and appeal. The plots and buildings of early Georgetown were rustic and utilitarian in character, and artifacts found at the site in the 1950s revealed no grand pleasure garden, only a dirt yard where chickens and pigs had free range.

The garden today is the product of one man's toil and dedication. After a four-year stint in the U.S. Air Force, Hunsaker, a gardener by avocation, attempted to find work in Washington to avoid the only other future facing him: a factory job in his native, hardscrabble Appalachia. Resigned to a life in a coal processing plant, he had packed all his belongings in his car to return to his native West Virginia, but on his way out of town he approached a National Park Service gardener at a small downtown park, got advice on finding a Park Service position, and abandoned his journey west. Much of his apprenticeship was spent at the White House Rose Garden, where a series of head gardeners taught him his craft. He came to the Old Stone House in 1976 and set about turning a lawn with sparsely planted trees into the flower garden that today continues to evolve and expand.

Although digging and planting the beds took six seasons, Hunsaker knew from the start that he wanted the type of decorative herbaceous borders that developed. The style looks to the past in its allusion to the English herbaceous border, but Hunsaker was also ahead of prevailing tastes in his luxuriant use of heritage roses and hardy perennials since rediscovered by a new generation of American gardeners. The plants thrive through deep, rich humus, replenished each year. The rejection of chemical sprays produces an abundant array of animals, from the five resident cats to butterflies and birds.

For his part Hunsaker finds the greatest solace soon after dawn, when he arrives. The plants are bejeweled by dew, the flock of goldfinches has yet to be frightened away by visitors, and the garden has a sublime stillness.

*H*ot spots of color burst forth from fields of milky white phlox, blue drifts of forget-me-nots, and other cottage plantings throughout the garden. Opposite, above: A showy pink single rose peers from one of the beds. Opposite, below: Roses of varied lineage and form are used extravagantly in partnership with herbaceous perennials. Left: The loose and abundant approach of the perennial borders gives the impression of a rich country cottage garden a world apart from the city outside.

ONE HUNDRED GARDENS

From a purely physical standpoint, the garden of Joseph and Polly Krakora functions supremely well: its introspective form and shady aspect offer a space that is intimate but not confined, soothing but never dull. Beyond its physical effect, however, the garden invites its friends to enter a world of fantasy and meditation spawned by the fertile imagination of its creator. Since the mid-1980s Joseph Krakora has built on its inward-looking qualities to create myriad miniature gardens—"a garden of a hundred gardens," he says, exaggerating only slightly. Hundreds of tiny algae fern floating in a stone vessel might be a vast lotus pond; a misshapen sprig of Japanese holly suggests a gnarled, wind-sculpted Japanese black pine, and a patch of quarter-inch partridge berry rises like a mass of hosta above a carpet of moss.

Dozens of such microscopic scenes feed the imagination and allow the Krakoras to surmount the centuries-old dilemma of the city garden—the lack of space. Creating this Lilliputian world is an old trick of Chinese and Japanese gardeners and long used to varying effect in the West. The vignettes are enjoyed in isolation, in sequence, and in interrelation; ultimately they recede, and the garden is viewed as a single composition of restrained order, from the progressive range of plant scale to the economical and unifying use of color.

Joseph Krakora is many things: vice president of the National Gallery of Art, film producer, former director of theater and opera, and graduate of New York's Union Theological Seminary. The garden has become another component of his creative sojourn. "All my jobs have been project oriented and focused on the creative process, and the garden is both," he says. "Creating is learning how to see things."

Aided by noted Georgetown landscape designer Jane MacLeish, he set to work soon after the Krakoras purchased the Federal rowhouse in 1985. The original structure, enlarged in 1870, dates to around 1783. An immediate task was to do something about three ancient, overgrown yews along the end of the side alley where the main garden space is announced. Krakora saved the yews and reclaimed the space by limbing them up (removing the lower branches) to reveal their ornamental bark and the interlapping architecture of the trunks.

Krakora wanted the sound of water in the garden, but the existing T-shaped pool was mute and jutted into the heart of the space. Again he and Jane MacLeish made something new from the old, keeping just the top of the T and placing an offset, higher pool behind. Now, the water roils in the rear section before falling in broad sheets over a copper lip to the lower half. The basket-weave brick terrace at the center of the garden was removed and reconfigured with the same brick, moss side up; the moss has since spread for the

*S*pace and scale are molded differently here to create a paradise as fertile as the imagination. Opening page: The sound of water resonates over the broad copper lip of the reworked pool. Detail: Polly Krakora's daughter, captured in childhood, adorns the tranquil garden. Opposite, above: Old millstones are laid flat or on edge to define minigardens. Opposite, below: A stone orb anchors a view of foliage. Left: The sculpture Sundance *draws the eye diagonally through the garden and its tunnel of graceful dogwoods.*

desired effect. Six flowering dogwoods, *Cornus florida*, were planted in a grid that frames the terrace and pool, and a seventh was positioned in the far northeast corner of the garden. The four on the south side mirror four existing hemlocks in a cultivated bed widened to align with the side of the house.

At the base of the hemlocks are cherry laurels, but much of the bed is bare, black soil in winter. From this oft-weeded minimalist ground plane, devoid of the inevitable mulch, islands of trillium and ferns emerge and grow through the spring. The white flowers of trillium bloom until late spring, when the cherry laurel, dwarf azaleas, and the dogwood all produce their own white blossoms. The white flowers tie the ground plane to the dogwood canopy and along with the garden's various shades of green provide a fresh, sophisticated aura. The bed on the other side of the central terrace is anchored by the other dogwoods underplanted with islands of azaleas and pachysandra. To the left of the pool Joseph Krakora has placed an abstract metal sculpture—

Free of excessive plant ornament and color, the garden coaxes a reflective response. Opposite: Sunbeams burst through the gaps in the stockade fence at dawn to unify the disparate forms of plant, stone, and brick. Left: A petrified nautilus provides a stone ornament typically unusual for this garden of many gardens.

35

*F*rom windswept mountains to craggy jungles, the garden evokes flights of fancy. *Right:* Sun-dappled moss suggests a cool forest floor. *Opposite, above:* Tiny algae fern float freely in a stone bowl. *Opposite, below:* A grind-stone centers one of the Krakoras' multitude of minigardens.

Sundance, by David Smalley. A second garden sculpture, of a child kneeling with cupped hands, was modeled by Charles Parks on Polly's daughter, Mary.

With the garden's bones in place, Joseph Krakora set about finding the smaller artifacts and plants that make up his landscapes of the mind. Many old bricked, shady gardens are naturally dank, and he saw this as a strength, a microclimate for mosses, ferns, and cultivated weeds, such as partridge berry and pennywort, that draw us into his fantasy. Many of the little gardens are anchored by an artifact—a nineteenth-century iron cauldron, now a centerpiece of the side garden and home to a white-flowering water lily; small grindstones, laid flat or on edge; Japanese rice-flour stones, similar in size but decorated with patterns on each side; a full-sized millstone used as a bench; huge natural stones, smooth, pitted, and deep gray, and placed at strategic spots; stone bowls; an antique stone Japanese lantern from Kyoto; and in one dogwood a delicate wind chime collected on one of his many visits to Japan and made by a family whose ancestors manufactured armor more than fifty generations earlier. They surely would be happy to find their chime in such a meditative space, where minimalist landscaping has cleared the head as much as the ground.

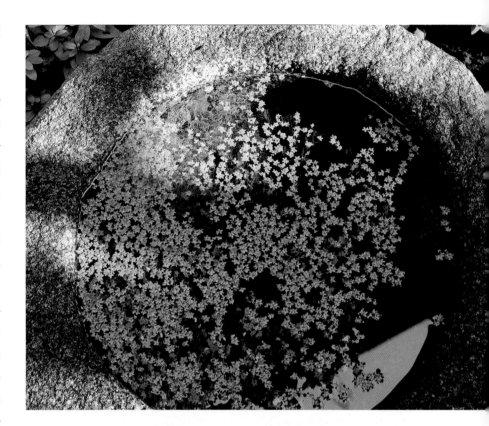

Joseph Krakora's gentle, kindly way masks the passion and drive that are the mark of true gardeners. He cannot pass a plant nursery without venturing in to seek out that one plant whose individual quirkiness would fit a predetermined spot. His ferns are vigorous and unusual, among them the Japanese holly fern and the shield fern, and he counts fifteen kinds of mosses. Wisteria and clematis drape the garden's brick walls except for the back wall, which is left clear as a canvas for the light. In winter and summer the old brick takes on a mellow golden glow; in spring, when the dogwoods flower, the garden takes on the freshness of youth, especially under clear, moonlit skies.

There are gardens of more superficial drama but none more honest. In a garden where space is expanded by the imagination, Joseph Krakora's magical journey has only just begun.

$\mathcal{A}$ CONSTANT VISION

In early March, when the first scent of spring is in the air, Eddie Allen can be found planting seeds in the greenhouse at Evermay. Some will grow into leathery begonias, others lush tomato vines, but the ritual is greater than the sum of its parts. It means that the great cycle of life has begun anew at the last great private estate in Georgetown, started at the beginning of the nineteenth century. Allen's tiny seeds are an affirmation that a house and garden claimed by the Belin family in 1923 continues on, season to season, year to year, generation to generation. Sited high in wooded seclusion, bordering a creek valley and a cemetery, Evermay enjoys commanding views east to official Washington. The distant office buildings of Foggy Bottom tell of the notorious transience of government officials and workers in the capital city. Evermay, by contrast, is a place where the constancy of one clan is as palpable a feature as the brick house and its formal gardens.

Evermay remains the embodied vision of its twentieth-century creator, F. Lammot Belin, who with his wife, Frances, restored the 1801 mansion to its Federal splendor. Similarly, the gardens are the fruit of his lucid sense of space and the inspiration of his world travels. Some features are clean and modern, others classical or exotic, but together they form a cohesive landscape of mystery and beauty.

When he came to it, Georgetown was a sorry sort of place, lost between its forgotten past and its uncertain future. The Victorians had done odd things to grand old houses. Coarse and unsettling architectural appendages had been added, and landscapes were little more than raw, sloping land with sparse plantings of trees or straggly shrubs. Such was Evermay when Mott Belin first set eyes on it. His friend and fellow diplomat Robert Woods Bliss mentioned over lunch at Dumbarton Oaks that Evermay was on the market. They sauntered over together, knocked on the door, and by afternoon's end Belin had presented a check to the proprietor.

The pace with which Belin, who had ties to the du Pont family, set about restoring and transforming the estate is remarkable. Work began in early January 1924, and by the month's end workers had removed Victorian additions and added the dormers on the roof. In February sixteen layers of paint had been removed to reveal the original hand-formed brick. The new west wing (the servants quarters) was already up to the second floor. By the end of March the frame for the wooden orangery was in place on the east side of the house; the high brick perimeter wall was well under way, and the major terracing work had begun on the grounds. By July the five-bay orangery was glazed with arching Palladian windows, the Italianate fountain terrace (later reworked) was built, and work was almost complete on the fifteen-foot-high brick wall separating the house's immediate

*P*layful figures of ancient mythology bolster Evermay's enchanted feel. Opening page: Spring blossoms induce water fights in the Cherub Fountain Garden. Detail: An angel marks a family columbary. Right, above: Native dogwoods brighten the spring landscape. Right, below: Brick was used for the path leading to the formal lower terraces and the cherub pool. Opposite: Marble and brick terraces pay homage to the mansion.

40

grounds from what became the vegetable and cutting gardens below.

An aerial photograph from around 1930 shows the domed Georgian-style temple at the east end of the formal lawn terrace, the Cherub Fountain Garden along the lower terrace to the south, and the boxwood shrubs (delivered by barge to the Georgetown harbor) forming an arching hedge on each end of the house. Still to come were the Rabat Fountain Garden, the Chinese pavilion overlooking the tennis court, the planted hillside down to the court, and the lawn on the east end of the Cherub Fountain Garden.

Thirty years later Belin, who had retired as ambassador to Poland in 1933, completed his last great work. Supervised by his son, Navy Capt. Peter Belin, the project encompassed the construction of a huge retaining wall between the property and Oak Hill Cemetery, the reconstruction of the orangery in brick to provide a balancing wing to the house, and the building of the fabulous walled forecourt, with its fountain by the great Swedish sculptor Carl Milles.

From the earliest days the formal earthworks were softened by layers of shade and evergreen trees, choice shrub specimens, and planted gardens of boxwood, azaleas, roses, and perennials. The vegetation included an elm grove on the south lawn terrace (of which only one tree survives), a heavy screen of conifers on the west side, southern magnolias near the house, and choice specimen conifers such as the blue atlas cedar near the temple and a rare oriental spruce in a grove near the forecourt. The spruce stands near a border of camellias in a color medley of carmine pink, shell pink, and creamy white blossoms. Together, the overstory of trees conveys the sense of a country house, which is what Evermay was when its first owner, Samuel Davidson, built it. Described as "a Scot of original character," Davidson also was shrewd, for he made money selling swampland to the government to build the White House while keeping a choice perch in Georgetown for himself.

Peter and Mary Belin, who became the owners after Mott Belin's death in 1961, understood their role in Georgetown and the importance to the community of preserving both the house and the grounds.

Wisteria, despite its infuriating reluctance to bloom, remains a favorite plant in Georgetown. Right: The white-flowering variety here has never failed to bloom, a fact put down to Mott Belin's regular feedings from his martini glass. Opposite: The landing of the south terrace invites pause between house and grounds.

ott Belin's tastes spanned the ages and civilizations. Opposite, far left: Classical ornament throughout the garden is rich, as can be seen in this figure on the stone bench. Opposite: The materials and workmanship are of a high order, as the copper-domed temple testifies. Left: Belin surpassed himself with the Rabat Fountain, crafted in Italy from his own field drawings of the original in the Moroccan capital.

Springtime visitors invariably find the lower lawn terrace awash in the first colors of the azalea season and are drawn to the old, floriferous wisteria draped over the temple. The balcony affords a splendid view of the city and the sunken Rabat Fountain Garden. To the right is a winding woodland path where the forest floor is carpeted with yellow-flowering lamiastrum that open unexpectedly onto a grassy terrace linking the woodland to another great formal work, the Cherub Fountain Terrace. The orchard beckons from beyond, on to the tennis court and its richly detailed Chinese viewing pavilion. Evermay is a garden for all seasons, but the nearby placement of peonies, old rugosa roses, and the powerfully fragrant calycanthus shrub bring color and scent in spring to this quiet corner of the estate.

Harry Belin, Peter's son, is a third-generation family member who lives in one of the houses on the estate. Among his most vivid memories are those of his summer jobs in the garden during his high school years, working for his grandfather's British gardener, Fred Joiner. "He claimed to smoke cigars for two reasons," says Harry Belin. "To keep the gnats away and to make insecticide" from chewed cigar butts mixed with water. "It was horrible to deal with, but it worked."

The most enchanting garden room encloses the Rabat Fountain Garden. Crafted in Italy in the late 1930s from a warm-toned marble, the fountain's opposing shell-like bowls spill into a long pool. The space's old, clipped American hollies seem to rest on slender classical columns recessed behind them. The west side of the garden is enclosed by the brick and balustraded retaining wall alongside the temple above and softened by banks of old azaleas. This is Mott Belin's masterful recreation of the Islamic water garden, an introspective and meditative space nourished by simple forms and the gentle sound of water.

Mott Belin lived to see the crowning glory of his beloved Evermay—work on the new orangery and forecourt garden. Like the Moorish-style Rabat Garden, this is a garden room created around a single work: a fluted, black granite fountain by Carl Milles, the focal point of a broad, circular pool coped in black marble and set in a court paved with pink granite blocks arranged in fan shapes. The whole space is defined by a decorative brick wall swagged between pillars. The crispness of the elements conveys a Modern style, but the organic presence of the fountain and its perfect proportion within its space bring a timeless beauty in complete sympathy with that of the house.

By decorating his gardens with the work of human beings Belin sought to place humankind not above nature but within it. The crafted beauty of the garden, in turn, uplifts the soul. That is the essence of Evermay, and ever may it be.

For all its exotic touches, Evermay retains an American character. Right: Native beauties such as this pink-flowering dogwood help create this sense of an old American garden. Opposite, above: The north forecourt is dominated by the muscular, fluted fountain by the brilliant Swedish sculptor Carl Milles. Opposite, below: Double columns appear to support great walls of American holly in the Rabat Fountain Garden.

FRENCH CONNECTIONS

In some gardens in Georgetown, no doubt, the outdoor space is designed and planted by one person and tended by another. This hands-off garden making may appeal to city dwellers whose links to the land have been long severed, but not to Brewster and Stephany Knight. Together they have spent the past few years turning their secluded, side-lot garden into a landscape of retreat and romance. It is a theater where the stage is of basket-weave brick and the backdrop is high, soothing green trellis work. Colorful plantings and the passage of the seasons provide changing scenery. And the drama itself? Sometimes it is glimpses of a childhood in France or imagined scenes of gardens in literature. But always it is a paradise that touches the heart. "When I was a little girl the book that most impressed me was *The Secret Garden,*" says Stephany Knight. Here, behind Georgetown's cobbled streets, she has taken a leaf out of Frances Hodgson Burnett's book and created her own "haven in a heartless world."

Built in 1803 and enlarged to the rear in the 1860s, the Knights' painted brick townhouse once fronted the street. In the 1950s the then-owner purchased the vacant lot on the east side to build a swimming pool and changed the house's orientation to the newly acquired land. The successful transformation provided a private facade with a period-style front door balanced on either side by French doors, similarly arched.

Unlike other side-lot properties, the house and garden seem melded together. The house is entered through the garden gate up a flight of steps. When the Knights first saw the property, the garden's spaciousness and the house's architecture immediately suggested their beloved France. As a girl Stephany Knight lived near Lyons, and Brewster Knight's grandfather and great-grandfather—the painters Aston and Ridgway Knight—lived and worked in Paris and Normandy. The way the facade of the Georgetown house presents itself, uninterrupted and at an angle, recalls the cottage of his father, Ambassador Ridgway Knight, south of Calais. The Knights themselves once lived in Paris. "For both of us," she says, that first sight induced "a rush of memories of friends and childhood and adulthood in France. We made up our minds as we stood in the garden to buy the house." The garden that emerged is not a facsimile of the French landscape. While it looks to Europe and California, it is a Georgetown home for a Georgetown life: elegant but not flashy, worldly yet American, sophisticated but not stuffy.

Both Knights bring their own passions to the garden. Stephany Knight planned most of the plant arrangements in the garden's diverse collections of clay pots. In those at the foot and top of the garden steps she has grown a small upright juniper softened at its feet with dainty variegated trailing ivy, pulmonaria, trailing vinca, and, for color, pastel

The Knights' passion for gardening extends from their private world to the street front of their 1803 home. Opening page: The entrance steps are softened and adorned with colorful annuals while trailing vinca veils the painted brick stair wall. Detail: A lion's-head fountain offers visual relief from bare Georgetown walls. Right: Garden furniture establishes the main entertainment space. Opposite: The garden becomes a natural extension of the house as well as a balance to its mass.

pink impatiens. Similar thoughtful compositions are seen elsewhere. The plant palette changes: smaller pots contain pelargonium while the larger pots hold woody plants such as nandina and rose of Sharon and others harbor herbaceous peonies and irises. Trailing ivy and vinca are used liberally, and their speckled forms shine in the garden's shady corners. The pots and garden borders alike are illuminated by masses of pastel-colored annuals, typically sky blue petunias and double-flowering impatiens in whites and light pink. The pots are arranged to designate subrooms within the long terrace, much as tables and vases might subdivide an interior room.

Brewster Knight's garden pursuits often are more prosaic. A visitor might find him stooped over a workbench, a pencil behind his ear, figuring out how to build the wooden fanlight segments he installed above the house entrances. His wife once found him smearing muriatic acid on his precious fountain statue of a vestal virgin. It was a desperate, final—and ultimately successful—effort to induce a patina of moss and algae. He also has responsibility for the house's facade, where he has created narrow beds for boxwood and climbing plants that have grown and curled around wall openings. Clematis, the climbing

rose 'New Dawn', and climbing hydrangea drape the latticed panels.

Brewster Knight's practical bent, however, does not obscure his own sense of the garden's sentimental powers. Before summer dinner parties, of which there are many, he will go to great trouble to light this verdant stage. Certain lights in the house will be turned on for effect, including a top-floor closet light. The garden lights will burn softly, enhanced by a liberal supply of candles. A pair of wrought-iron outdoor candelabra each burn three fat candles in the gathering corner defined by the fountain and an array of padded iron chairs, chaise longues, and tables. Classical music, as well as food and wine, completes the mood. "Very theatrical," muses Stephany Knight. "This is the artistic side of Brewster."

The garden today gives little clue to its condition in 1985, when the Knights first saw and fell in love with it. The pool had long been bricked over, and the garden walls were formed by an impenetrable screen of bamboo, which created privacy but had grown thick and was home to dozens, perhaps hundreds, of European starlings. Now, decorative, high trellis fencing painted in a quiet deep green that recedes with the afternoon shadows surrounds the garden. It has become a gracious background for a row of hop-hornbeams that frames the far side of the garden, underpinned by clipped Merserve holly. The two ends of the garden are planted with espaliered Burford holly, and the end with the corner fountain is softened further by massed oakleaf hydrangea.

The garden's far end is cast into even greater darkness by the presence of a towering double-trunk American holly wrapped in a green, iron circular bench. This is a cool, out-of-the way place for hot summer afternoons, made more inviting by a hammock at one end.

The garden's design is not yet final. Future possibilities include installing a small classical pool in the style of one at Dumbarton Oaks and adding fragrant plants to create another dimension to the dinner party stage set. In the Knights' secret garden the course toward magic and innocence is slow and wandering. The joy is not so much in reaching journey's end but the sojourn through the memories of far-off places and a distant childhood.

Stephany Knight tends to the pots while Brewster is on patina patrol. Opposite: Acid-induced algae climb the vestal virgin. Left: Subgardens are formed with groupings of richly planted clay pots. A joyful mixture of annuals and herbs is gathered beneath a budding rose of Sharon. This container landscaping is demanding work in a harsh microclimate, but the reward is sweet, especially during candlelighted dinner parties in the garden.

ROMANCE OF THE ROSE

From Georgetown's earliest days the choicest sites for homes and gardens were in the northeast section of the settlement. Here, the rocky land rose steeply and offered handsome locations for grand houses, splendid views, and a country ambiance. Estates such as Evermay, Tudor Place, and Dumbarton Oaks were far removed physically and emotionally from the noises, smells, and tawdry bustle of the river port. About 1805 one property owner resisted the urge to follow the pack and built an unassuming gabled brick cottage of consummate charm and rustic honesty. The expansive site has shrunk over the years, but the Smith-Winslow House's south-facing veranda and fluid gabled roof line have kept its picturesque character intact.

It is the perfect setting for a romantic cottage garden, and, happily, it has one—not a wild one but a refined and civilized version. Lavender, rosemary, herbaceous peonies, and clematis speak to the sophistication of garden and gardener alike, but it is another plant that sets this garden so much apart—the rose.

Rose gardens are rare in Georgetown and for good reason. Poor air circulation, the heat-island effect of the city, and small shady sites conspire against this favored but fussy plant. Here, however, the rose garden is reclaimed through the use of old-fashioned rose shrubs and climbers or their derivatives. The owner has discovered what many gardeners today have forgotten: old roses are more disease resistant than modern types and produce flowers of unsurpassed beauty and fragrance.

One refreshing aspect of this garden is the extravagant use of vigorous climbers on the walls of both the house and the carriage house–garage. If foundation plants hide a building, climbing plants glorify it, yet they are often rejected by owners cautious about drilling holes into mortar or weatherboard and worried about having to repaint trellises and climbing high to prune them. As this garden demonstrates, however, this extra step can produce sublime results. In May the east side of the house is smothered in hundreds of sweetly fragrant light-pink blossoms of the climber 'Mme. Alfred Carriere', borne by three old but well-pared plants. The carriage house, delightful in form and proportion, is similarly draped. The sunny south-facing wall is covered in the medium-pink blossoms of the popular climber 'New Dawn', underplanted with the gallica 'Rosa Mundi', with its peculiar striped petals. Above the carriage house's west-facing doors the tiny white blossoms of the prolific 'Kiftsgate' rose open two to three weeks later. It is pruned at least once a year to keep it in bounds; unfettered, it will climb seventy feet or more when mature.

A fence dividing the carriage-house side garden from the swimming pool terrace is draped with the old-fashioned tea rose 'Sombrueil'

Roses provide the life force in this garden of refined rustic delight. Opening page: White pickets and paving stones set the mood of romance and mystery. Detail: Rambling roses form a bower of color and scent during the garden's late spring climax. Opposite: The porch is a triumph of the carpenter's skills and offers a cool and breezy retreat. Left: The side white garden earns its name from the profusion of the floribunda 'Iceberg'.

while a free-standing bower in the little garden is given height and focus with the wichuraiana climber 'May Queen'.

The effect of roses lumbering over painted brick recalls the small chateau gardens of northern France, although the owner's inspiration and tastes are shaped by influences much closer to home—her mother's old-rose gardens in Virginia and Maine.

The garden has always been important to this house—the previous owner was an avid gardener before the current owners moved here in 1977—but undoubtedly the beauty of the landscape today has been brought about by a masterful reconfiguration of the land. For most of its life the house looked south—the main entrance was through the veranda—and its driveway snaked up the hill from the street a block below. Over the years, because of such additions as a full-sized tennis court, the arrival side of the house shifted to the north side, off a quiet side street. Architect Joanne Goldfarb saw the need to create a more worthy entrance and hide a nearby basement door. Today, a

*T*he architect's period-style carriage house–garage reorganized garden spaces and provided a host for spectacular climbers and ramblers. *Right: This scene is captured once a year: the vigorous 'New Dawn' will repeat, not so the pinker 'May Queen' to the right and the 'Rosa Mundi' at its feet. Opposite, above: The roses are carried forth into the next garden terrace, an open sunny space for cooler months. Opposite, below:* Buddleia alternifolia offers a long and showy display of pink flowers.

The owner has sliced up the landscape to create a series of intimate spaces that call to mind Victorian drawing rooms. Broadleaf evergreens function as walls, pea gravel as the rug, and patio furniture as table and chairs. Allium, roses, and peonies provide the chintz. The garden's air of casual brilliance belies the commitment that such a colorful landscape demands.

handsome brick stairway, augmented with a wooden balustrade, a landing, and a portico, announces the house and hides the reorganized steps to the basement. Before it lies a new forecourt of exposed aggregate concrete in bands of brick. But the master stroke is the carriage house–garage, which replaced an old carport on the other end of the forecourt. The new building might be for a horseless carriage, but it is faithful to its Federal progenitors in scale, materials, and appearance, although a fanlight takes the place of the typical hoist beam above the doors.

In addition to its sympathetic beauty, the garage brought a pleasing rearrangement of the garden rooms. The forecourt extends to the area of the old carport and is delineated with a stand of hornbeams. Behind it is a small garden room of intimacy and delight. Brightened by a floor of pea gravel, it is announced by an arch carrying another 'May Queen' rose. Inside, the garden is edged in beds of rosemary, peonies, lesser perennials, and more roses. The carriage house screens a neighbor's house and sets up the adjoining small garden, which, in turn, leads to the expansive pool terrace. It is screened by clipped broadleaf evergreen trees and conifers, and its formality dovetails with the rustic charm of the path to a lower garden, marked by a specimen Japanese maple of great age and character. The veranda view picks up this naturalistic feel with a grove of pink-flowering dogwoods; on summer mornings they filter the sun and make the veranda an especially agreeable spot to sit and read.

The narrow garden on the west side of the house is a pleasant woodland shade garden, but its dominating feature is an ancient oak said to be the oldest tree in Georgetown. It is a fitting companion to the house and a fixture in a garden where change is the constant for a gardener who loves to move or replace plants that do not perform.

Architect Goldfarb harbors fond memories of the property. "It's just a really nice nineteenth-century farmhouse that in the American style has developed and changed." Happily, the changes have refined the property without altering its spirit as a splendid country house in the city.

THE POWER GARDEN

Politicking is a science in Washington's corridors of government. In the Georgetown garden it has long been cultivated as an art. The amorphous commodity of power is traded gently in the relaxed, off-hours setting of boxwood and brick. The tradition not only thrives; in recent years it has been elevated to new heights by Georgetown's most celebrated contemporary hostess, Pamela Harriman.

Week in and week out, as many as five hundred guests might file through the Federal townhouse and into the multiterraced garden for dining and entertainment. Beyond her fund-raising efforts for the Democratic Party, Harriman is credited with playing a key role in reshaping Democratic politics in the fallow years of the 1980s and setting the stage for the party's return to power in 1992. In the weeks after his election, Bill Clinton made only a few expeditions out of Arkansas, but one of them was to Pamela Harriman's home.

In her mission Harriman's garden has become a full partner. But the secluded landscape is more than a political ally. In its private, quiet mood, stripped of the tents, portable wooden floors and stages, cocktail bars, and buffet tables, it is a friend to a woman whose life journey has taken many different and far-flung turns but has never strayed far from the garden path. "I have always been lucky enough to live with gardens," she says. "I can't imagine a life without gardens."

Harriman's father, Lord Digby, created one of Britain's great rhodo-dendron gardens at Minterne, a Dorset estate landscaped in the arcadian style of Capability Brown. The former daughter-in-law of Sir Winston Churchill and later the wife of statesman and former New York Gov. W. Averell Harriman, she has been close to the leading political figures of her day and now is one herself, as ambassador to France.

Harriman's Georgetown garden (she has others in Middleburg, Virginia, and the Bahamas) consists of five terraces that bring formal order and calm to an otherwise steep change of elevation. Each terrace has its own character, yet together they present a unified whole. The upper dining terrace, with its carpet of granite, is stiff and formal; the parterre terrace continues the strong plant architecture but is made more relaxed by its greater breadth and brick paving; the lawn terrace is softened by beds of looser plant material; the pool terrace brings fluid balance to the hardscape; and the lowest tier is given a shady and faintly tropical feel through thick stands of bamboo and southern magnolias.

Delightful and unexpected plant combinations are found in pockets of the landscape—primulas, pansies, and painted ferns, for example—but this is essentially an architectural garden. The plants are woody and take their cue from red brick and flecked granite. Previously each spring the garden was awash with twenty-five hundred multicolored tulips, but in recent seasons the grounds have become more subdued. Along

the lawn terrace's erstwhile tulip border, for example, the emphasis has turned from spring to autumn, when massed plantings of *Arum italicum* emerge at the feet of the towering grass, *Miscanthus sinensis gracillimus.* As the grass turns its winter straw color, distant pyracanthas of great age burst into color with their red berries. Flowering trees offer their own beacons to the season: star and saucer magnolias in March and April, southern magnolias in June, and crape myrtles in July and August.

Even when it is too hot or too cold or too wet to be in the garden, Pamela Harriman is never far from it, thanks to a large and airy conservatory built on the site of an old frame porch. To the side, the conservatory's supports frame a canvas of plant texture—the foliage of the trees and shrubs across the dining terrace, among them Japanese cryptomeria planted by Averell Harriman, southern magnolia, willow, osmanthus, and variegated pieris. The conservatory's far end appears to jut above the next terrace down. One has the sense of being on the prow of a ship, looking down on the calm waters of boxwood.

The sunroom is filled with cut flowers and potted plants brought down from the cutting gardens and greenhouses in Middleburg, among them dracaenas with slender trunks and arching leaves, a ficus plant with a braided trunk, and kalanchoes blooming rose and yellow. A planter might contain sprays of speckled, chartreuse orchids. In the adjoining room of the house visitors find a continuous display of white roses.

The house was built in 1813–16 by Romulus Riggs, and for most of the nineteenth century it was the home and classroom of Dr. Joshua Riley, one of Georgetown's preeminent physicians; for years afterwards it was known as "old Doctor Riley's place." The property has been enlarged and lovingly gardened. Perry Wheeler, the landscape architect, refined the plantings over time; before his involvement the landscape design team of Rosemarie Edmunds, later the wife of noted architect Grosvenor Chapman, and Sarah Hitchcock, now Yerkes, added evergreen trees and shrubs, reworked the stone steps, and designed the

An architectural garden of terraces strikes a balance between the social demands and the private role of the house. Opening page: The enclosed porch brings the garden inside. Potted kalanchoes flower within, while a distant star magnolia outside flags the start of spring. Detail: Bicolored pansies grow amid Japanese painted ferns. Opposite: Crape myrtle branches form elegant tracery against the main steps. Left: The plumes of the miscanthus grass and great clusters of orange pyracantha fruit speak at season's end of nature's fertility.

swimming pool terrace. After the assassination of President Kennedy, Averell Harriman, then under secretary of state, lent the home to Jacqueline Kennedy and her children. They lived there until Mrs. Kennedy bought her own home in the neighborhood.

Fame returned to old Doctor Riley's place as it became the center of Pamela Harriman's partisan milieu. Even as she guided the house to new political and social heights, however, the garden remained her own retreat, a place to catch her breath in an increasingly hectic schedule or take a dip in the heated pool. It is a garden well suited to its dual role.

The garden's tiered descent and screening by structures and plants allow distinguished guests, among them Bill Clinton and Raisa Gorbachev, to visit in absolute seclusion. Opposite: During large gatherings the lower main terrace becomes a cocktail party room. Left: The utilitarian pool house is masked by rambling roses and container plantings of seasonal annuals.

*T*he architectural character of
the garden allows easy transition
from private to party and fits
with its urban setting. Right: The
path to the heated swimming pool
is well traveled, even in winter.
For parties, the potted jasmine in
the boxwood knot are removed
to make room for a stage. Opposite:
A saucer magnolia lights the way
to Harriman's adjoining
office garden.

$\mathcal{W}$INDING RIBBONS

A straight line might be the shortest distance between two points, but in the garden of this attractive Federal townhouse the curved line leads directly to the heart. Bands of plant color, winding ribbons of limestone, and the sensuous curves of a double staircase of stone lend a fluid grace to a garden set within the otherwise severe lines of the walled yard.

The garden was designed and built in the early 1980s, when the house underwent extensive renovations. The owners were committed to a high level of refinement and detail inside and out and for the garden found their soul mate in the young, gifted landscape architect David Campbell. He died soon after its completion at the age of thirty-three. One can only wonder how his work would have evolved, but this garden speaks to an already well-developed passion for classical elements, a delight in visual illusions, and the attention to detail that has remained the hallmark of his company, DCA Landscape Architects.

The same virtues are seen on the public side of the house, although in a more subdued form. Spring visitors might find hundreds of pansies at the foot of the street tree, a Norway maple, in beguiling pastel shades anchored by others in purple and deep mauve. Clipped American hollies screen the first-floor interior while forcing the eye up the curving front stairs, where a custom-made lead planter houses a dwarf conifer shod in ivy and trailing purple-flowering lantana. The four-story brick house, one of five townhouses in Smith Row, was built about 1815–16 and is considered among the most splendid architecture in the urban village. Its austere Federal facade is loosened by Regency swags in recessed panels and by the Tudor rose motif on the window lintels.

The design of the rear garden was shaped by alterations to the house. A cozy breakfast room was added, from which one enters the garden. The basement was turned into a finished dining room that opens onto a shady sitting terrace, itself the result of extensive excavation and earth working. An oval of limestone is set into the flagstone terrace floor, but the double staircase encloses the space and gives it its dominant ornament. Ten steps on each side curve down and around the rusticated wall of the stairs. An arched niche houses a fish fountain above the exquisite lead-sided fountain pool, which in turn is straddled by two sweetbay magnolias, *Magnolia virginiana*, graceful small deciduous trees that do not hide the lines of the stonework.

The twisting stone banisters, the changing radii of the stone treads, and the thin, recessed lights in the risers all speak to the degree of detail and craftsmanship required to build the garden. Devising such a sheltered retreat in a lot that measures just thirty feet by sixty feet is not easy, yet it is accomplished without sacrificing the dominating presence of the main garden above.

Front and back, ironwork of a high order adds unusual grace to the house. Opening page: Clipped American hollies provide balance to the front of the Federal structure without imposing symmetry. The eye is led up the stairs by the decorative iron railing. Detail: Street plantings of pansies provide inviting color. Right: Interlocking ribbons of limestone throw the eye a curve. Opposite, above: Hand-forged railings reflect the garden's fluid grace. Opposite, below: The canal is brought out from the wall to allow a screen of delicate plum trees.

Again, detail and the curve are the key. The underlying linearity of the main garden is not ignored; indeed, it was reinforced by the reworked entrance to the carriage house–garage at the foot of the garden. White columns rise to support a classical arch above the door in a grand gesture that echoes the nobility of the house. The carriage-house entrance is the magnet that draws one through the garden, but the procession is halted by artful digressions, including the brass-railed iron staircase off the breakfast room, with its twisting form and ornament, an illuminated fountain and canal along the right wall, and the gentle steps up to the carriage house at garden's end.

At the point where the ribbons of limestone interweave in the paving, the designer established the cross-axis, again to slow the procession to garden's end and create a logical location for the specially designed garden furniture. The main feature of the cross-axis is the elaborate trompe l'oeil used to lengthen the space and address the problem of a large maple tree, which grows on the property line and interrupts the boundary wall.

On the opposite side of the garden the axis is taken to its conclusion with the placement of a lead swan fountain, behind which the canal curves into the wall. This flourish might easily have been right-angled, but the curving of the coping reinforces the garden's serpentine motif and again illustrates the eye for detail. By bringing the canal out from the wall, Campbell also allowed room for a bed of ornamental purple plum trees, underplanted with bulbs and annuals. The trees' petite, architectural qualities make them ideal for the limited space, and the rich purple foliage provides an exquisite foil for the various shades of green in the garden.

The beds on both sides provide the gaiety and color the owners wanted in carefully selected color schemes throughout the year: tulips in spring, annuals in summer, and chrysanthemums in fall. Even here, plants of different height and color are arranged in winding ribbons to reflect the weaving of architectural detail.

As a whole, the garden reflects the qualities that make Georgetown gardens so special: imaginative design, enduring craftsmanship, and in this case the simple curve, which the eighteenth-century landscaper Batty Langley described as nature's gift to humankind.

The landscape architect wanted finely crafted detail literally at every turn. Opposite: The curving stone steps melt into the fountain wall and embrace the shady retreat of the sunken garden. The stonework is in the best tradition of the collaborative art of the designer and mason. Left: The ornate terra-cotta pot holds its own against lavish container plantings.

$\mathcal{A}$ WASHINGTON LEGACY

Occupying one of the last remaining open landscapes in Georgetown, Tudor Place has kept the world at bay since 1816. The neoclassical mansion is both grand and austere, unlike any other in the capital: the brick, exposed in other houses of the time, is daubed in tan stucco, and its south front is adorned with a domed portico. Tudor Place was built to demonstrate the political allegiances and status of its owners and the taste of its architect, William Thornton, the first architect of the U.S. Capitol. But what sets it apart is the sustained care it has received from one family for nearly two hundred years.

The Peter family's relationship with the house began in 1802, when Martha Peter, a granddaughter of Martha Custis Washington, and Thomas Peter rented one of the two Georgian wings that predated Thornton's magnificent center block. George Washington left the Peters eight thousand dollars, which they used to buy the property and finish the house. In 1854 Tudor Place passed to the Peters' daughter Britannia Kennon—beautiful in youth, indomitable in spirit—who shepherded it through its most difficult years. To prevent its conversion into a Union hospital during the Civil War, Kennon, a southern sympathizer, grudgingly took in Union officers as boarders but insisted that the war not be discussed in her presence. The Peters had been close friends of Robert E. Lee, whose wife was Martha Peter's niece. Despite declines in the family fortunes, she resisted the impulse of other owners of large Georgetown tracts to subdivide the land for housing. Stewardship passed to her grandson, Armistead Peter, Jr., when she died at age ninety-six in 1911.

The new owner, with the help of his architect brother, refurbished the house in 1914, but it was his son, Armistead Peter III, who cared for the estate for most of this century and was responsible for the major landscaping improvements after his father's death in 1960. Before he died, in 1983, the last master secured Tudor Place's future by turning it over to the Tudor Place Foundation, which he established. Since then a professional gardening staff has brought the gardens and grounds up to probably the best level of care and ornament they have ever seen, and the garden has become one of Washington's horticultural jewels.

The house has two distinct personas, and the gardens reflect these accordingly. The south front, with its red-domed portico and balanced wings, is resplendent, and the grounds on the south side step back to give the grand facade its due. The north face, the carriage entrance, takes the Federal ideal of architectural plainness to the point of starkness; to compensate, the north side became the place for showy formal gardens.

A visitor first encounters a huge circle of billowing boxwood dating to Tudor Place's earliest days. Then a small hedge, this common

boxwood, *Buxus sempervirens,* today is big and fat and fills the air with its bittersweet scent, speaking to the estate's colonial and southern character. The circle marks the beginning of a long axis that once led the garden all the way up to R Street before the upper third of the estate was sold off in 1854.

The garden now features a well-proportioned flower knot garden, set in borders of old and new roses. The knot is patterned with low, clipped boxwood and fleshed out with the rose 'Gruss an Aachen', a delightful pastel pink against which facer plantings of blue, white, and silver perennials, including candytuft planted by Armistead Peter III and such later additions as dianthus, stachys, and campanula, are used to great effect.

The knot is another early feature of the garden, for ornamental pleasure gardens were as important to Martha Peter as the estate's orchards and vegetable plots. However, the boxwood in the knot garden was plundered during a four-year absence by Britannia Kennon, and the garden's design was thought lost until the 1920s, when her grandson and great-grandson found a book showing the Tudor Place knot garden reproduced at a relative's garden in Virginia. Armistead Peter III made other sympathetic additions to the north gardens, including the construction of the little Lion Fountain across a walk from the secret Circular Garden and extensive plantings in the three subgardens that make up the shady, green, and lush Tennis Court Garden, named for its incarnation as a tennis lawn.

Peter was trained in Paris as an artist but also proved an artful mason. In addition to the Lion Fountain, complete with a niche for fish to hide from raccoons, he built an area of intricate brick paving around a circular bench that overlooks a wilderness area on the western edge of the property. His greatest architectural success, however, was the Bowling Green, a sunken lawn edged with sloping sides and an enclosed south end brought to life with a lily pool. The view back takes the eye up an ivy-covered embankment, past a pair of lead greyhounds, to a pavilion on the northern edge of the property. The garden is entered through a path that curves around the large Bird Fountain, a lead

The domed portico of the Peter family's grand Federal mansion has been a Georgetown landmark for nearly two centuries. Opening page: Early spring brings bright drifts of daffodils, the scent of newly mown grass, and the promise of another glorious season at Tudor Place. Detail: White tulips lend their own freshness to the Thistle Garden. Opposite: The Tennis Court Garden today provides a peaceful, winding lawn edged with specimen trees and shrubs.

At each turn, a new garden
unfolds, different in scale and
mood from the last. Right: The
formal north gardens yield to a
woodland path edged in blue scilla
and cyclamineus daffodils.
Opposite: Woodland perennials
bring a delicate beauty to the floor
of a simple arbor. Dicentris, foam
flower, and ajuga are planted
in color combinations of mauve,
white, and blue.

work styled after a fountain motif of the Italian Renaissance. The Bowling Green Garden is one of the latest additions to the grounds, but from its setting and patina it might be the oldest. It is a study in green, except for a white-flowering deciduous magnolia in the early spring, and it retains its cool aura on the hottest summer day.

In a property of such continuum, trees take on a significance typically associated with timeless European gardens. By the Thistle Terrace visitors find a pecan tree planted by Britannia Kennon in 1875. During the same period she planted two copper beech saplings that grew to vast size on the north side of the house and became key garden landmarks before their recent demise. Three elms on the south lawn have perished, but other majestic shade trees flourish, including a white oak that sprouted from a locust stump around 1875 and grew into a specimen of rare size and sublime, spreading form. Another white oak on the northeastern boundary was planted in the late eighteenth century and now forms what Peter called a triad

with another white oak and a scarlet oak planted in this century.

The most visible work of the last owner of Tudor Place is the border trees and shrubs planted to screen the estate from neighboring blocks of houses. Originally the property was surrounded by wheat fields, and much of its south lawn was grown as a hay meadow until the advent of large mechanical mowers early this century. With surrounding development, Tudor Place lost its isolation and became something of a fishbowl. The screening plants do not detract from the garden's feel as an old East Coast property, and many of the understory shrubs have become fantastic specimens in their own right, including a broad, floriferous smokebush, *Cotinus coggygria,* on the lawn's west side.

Despite a limited number of herbaceous plantings, gardens of this size require an almost daunting degree of care and maintenance. The foundation has embraced the challenge with an eye to the future as well as the past. Some trees have been thinned, including a Japanese pagoda tree, *Saphora japonica,* which grew too large and began to shade the rose knot, and an American yellowwood weakened by borers. Changes will come slowly and gently. An enclosed lawn in the formal north gardens has been turned into an ornamental fruit garden, replacing a boxwood nursery and evoking the great plots of currant, gooseberry, and vegetables on the lost northern fringe of the estate. Efforts are under way to rebuild a wooden Gothic pavilion and transform the wilderness area to the northwest into a naturalistic dell with native shrubs, perennials, and bulbs.

There is no plan to freeze the garden in some representative period because there is none. It flourished and evolved at the hands of one family over a span of 181 years. Armistead Peter III, who, for all his extensive plantings and garden building, remained true to his forebears, wrote, "It has not any of the modern and expensive characteristics that one often finds in a garden. It is a simple garden, developed on the basis of shrubbery and trees in a way that I think my great-great-grandparents would have done if they had been faced with the same problems."

*T*he house and garden together create high drama in a showy setting, but there is nothing flashy or vulgar about Tudor Place. The estate's strength derives instead from the elegance of restraint. *Opposite, above: The mass of a lead urn is reduced through its unusual open-weave form. Opposite, below: Under-plantings are discreet and can be enjoyed from a distance or close up. Left: Southerners at heart, the Peters loved boxwood and used it freely. In spring its light green flush and fine texture create a perfect foil for darker, coarser vegetation.*

*T*he austere north front of the house shows the Federal style at its most plain. *Right: This architectural economy becomes a counterpoint to the showiest gardens. Opposite, above: The flower knot garden in midspring offers burgeoning roses underplanted with chartreuse euphorbias and lamb's-ears. Opposite, below: The rose 'Gruss an Aachen' unifies the varied plantings of perennials in each segment of the knot.*

$\mathscr{T}$ROMPE L'OEIL

Side-lot gardens in Georgetown present special problems—and opportunities—for the landscape architect. Design schemes that are too timid are dominated by the house; those too bold distract from it. The juxtaposition of house and garden generally requires an easy alliance between the two. Views from major rooms must provide interest and enticement, paths must flow freely between house and garden, and the garden's architectural details must relate to those of the house. All this is deftly achieved at the historic Crawford-Cassin House.

Named for its first two occupants, the house has been turning heads since it was built about 1816. Its three-story facade is of splendid Federal proportion and ornament, and its detached setting—back from and above the street—lends an air of aloofness softened by the pale yellow-painted brick. The garden wraps around three sides of the house, broadening to forty-five feet on the east side along the house's principal adornment: a double-deck porch. This veranda and the side garden itself suggest a southern setting and earlier had inspired a simple boxwood garden. It was removed in 1992, when new owners John and Patricia Figge directed a refurbishment indoors and out.

Landscape architect Yunghi Epstein and partner Joanne Lawson found the boxwood in poor health and, more to the point, the garden itself a stranger to the house. The old garden had some merit: namely,

four choice tree specimens on the east and southeast portions of the lot: three *Magnolia grandifloras*, one *Magnolia* x *soulangiana*, and a stunning Japanese maple, *Acer palmatum*. An existing clipped hedge of osmanthus provided a buffer between the grounds and the street below and also was retained. The new design was driven by several issues, the most problematic of which produced the most dramatic element in the landscape composition. The side garden, bounded by the porch and a neighbor's monolithic brick side wall, had become a canyon that funneled an unappetizing view of the rear yards of rowhouses one block north.

Epstein and Lawson devised a large garden pavilion set on the north end of the side garden that screens the view, connects two important axes, and gives focus and meaning to the side garden. It doubles as a garden house, provides a transition between the grand side garden and the more intimate rear garden, and through the use of trompe l'œil and a large reflecting mirror makes the side garden even longer, transforming it from adjunct space to esplanade. Crafted in redwood and painted white, the structure also relates to the house: its chamfered piers mirror those of the porch, and its open pediment recalls the building's classical references. Despite the high brick walls and the mature magnolias, the garden has an expansiveness rare in Georgetown, and the designers accordingly wanted a pavilion large

$\mathcal{S}$ide-lot gardens in George-town present the extra challenge of marrying the outdoor space to the interior. Opening page: Within a framework of existing old magnolias, the designers created an open, ceremonial side garden through subtle changes of level and crisp lines. Detail: A checkerboard fountain establishes a recurring motif and allows a water feature free of raccoons. Right: A statue of a young girl restores intimacy to the front garden. Opposite, above: From the porch the owners can view the beautiful autumn colors of Georgetown's street trees. Opposite, below: Grassed steps connect the dry pool to the grand trompe l'oeil pavilion.

enough to hold its own: its elevated floor is eleven feet square and the pediment rises to fifteen feet.

The porch stairs, formerly between the northernmost piers and aligned with the drawing room door, have been moved one bay south to produce a more interesting promenade from house to garden. The repositioning allowed Epstein and Lawson to create enough room between the pavilion and the terrace off the porch for a fountain garden in scale with its surroundings. When the fountain itself is on, three jets of water shoot up in their own recirculating wells hidden by squares of river stone. These in turn form part of a larger checkerboard of alternating flagstone and clipped Japanese holly squares. The motif is repeated at other points in the landscape, including the charming streetside garden, where flagstone squares in grass provide a resting point at the foot of one of the magnolias. Here a statue of a little girl humanizes the otherwise grand effect of the new side garden.

The side garden now is not only the central space but also a rather grand and ceremonial one. The edges under the great tree canopies have been underplanted with oakleaf hydrangeas, *Euonymus sieboldiana,* and banks of azaleas, placing the open, central promenade in starker relief. The borders flanking the fountain terrace have been made more dainty with flowering perennials, including astilbe, lythrum, sedum, and daylilies, but the pavilion behind sets the more august tone.

Intimacy is reserved for the rear garden, itself the solution to a visual hurdle. The bow window of the dining room looked out to the unappealing side wall of the garage. Epstein and Lawson designed a high trellised fence, but instead of placing it at the garden's perimeter, in front of the garage wall, they brought it forward eight feet to align with the back of the pavilion. This screened the garage, gave cars more room to turn at the garage entrance, and within the garden brought the whole scale down.

Here a straight path connects the back entrance of the house with the pavilion, planted on either side with small shrubs, perennials, and herbs in a color scheme of yellow, purple, and silver. The redwood

Ironically, illusion and a clear sense of space are the hallmarks of this garden. Right: The pavilion becomes a resting spot and a point of transition between the narrow kitchen path garden and the main garden. Opposite: The pavilion was crafted from redwood and then painted white to add to its already imposing stature. The designers wanted it to have an overriding presence in its canyon-like void. The back mirror gives further depth to the side garden.

trellis, stained the same dark Essex green as the house shutters, is draped with morning glories and clematis. Between the fence and the garage wall an improved cultivar of the callery pear, 'Aristocrat', provides further screening and a curtain of white blossoms in early spring.

The designers considered extending the fencing on the other side of the pavilion to enclose the northeast corner of the garden. But an old southern magnolia prevented this, and the obstacle yielded its own happy solution. Now, one traverses the herb garden path into the pavilion to discover a wonderful opening of space and light beyond, first to a wilderness garden of woodland shrubs and then to the borrowed view of neighbors' walled gardens.

In its rich diversity of plantings, scale, and mood, the Figge garden today pays homage to a splendid house and to Georgetown itself.

MAGNOLIA ALLÉE

The visitor enters the dark hallway of Richard and Katherine Bull's handsome Federal townhouse and is drawn by the allure of distant light: first the gentle glow of the drawing room, then the bright expanse of a large, modern kitchen, and on, inevitably, to the brilliance of the small south-facing garden. From Easter to November the garden is probably their favorite living space, used for breakfast, weekend lunches, and running space for a hound named Burghley. And here the Bulls can watch a carefully staged garden drama unfold.

The garden's elaborate structure—the raised flagstone terrace and the brick that decorates paving, walls, and the ornamental pool—suggests an architectural garden, but it is also the happy domain of a practicing gardener. No space is wasted: the small pool is inhabited by trout-sized koi; a sterile side yard becomes an allée of magnificent sheared magnolia; and in the darkest, out-of-the-way spots Katherine Bull has planted woodland shrubs and perennials of worldly charm. The melding of function and horticulture makes this a worthy city garden, but like all successful landscapes it has taken an enduring investment of time, vision, money, and love.

In 1974 the Bulls turned to Lucinda Friendly Murphy, descendant of a prominent Georgetown family and a landscape designer with experience in small city gardens. The Bulls' property was typical of many unimproved Georgetown lots of the day. The garden was physically and emotionally detached from the house (the Smith-Morton House, built 1818–19), wooden stairs led to a lawn edged with ugly metal fencing, and desolate, overgrown shade trees, including an old, dense Norway maple, were scattered randomly about. The designer replaced the lawn with a lower terrace of basket-weave brick and the fences with new board fencing to the west and a stepped, L-shaped perimeter brick wall on the south and east sides containing decorative panels in a herringbone pattern. Along the side yard Murphy proposed the *Magnolia grandiflora* as a bold solution to the problem of bringing life to an unyielding space while softening and screening the towering, windowless side wall of the adjoining house. These magnolias will grow one hundred feet high and perhaps fifty feet wide, but here they are wall-grown in the European manner; although they require tending, the effect is stunning. The leathery leaves draw the light into the side yard and deflect it, and in June the passageway is scented with the lemony fragrance of the beautiful, waxy white blossoms. The magnolia wall is sheared twice in the season. Every third or fourth spring the trees are pruned to bare wood; within three months the foliage is back, thick and glossy, and the flower buds that escaped the shears are ready to burst.

Murphy installed a series of raised beds at the edge of the main

Using every inch of growing space, and more, Richard and Katherine Bull have taken a small townhouse yard and turned it into a garden of rich bounty. From majestic hedges of southern magnolia to espaliered fruit trees, the palette seems distilled from a great country estate. Opening page: By the sitting terrace, ivy is trained into diamonds. Pots allow many more plants, including a handsome specimen of Rhododendron x 'Boule de neige'. *Detail: Crocus and scilla are bounded by a low bamboo fence. Right: Bulbs are important season openers. Tulips are arranged in waves, with later types at the front to mask spent early varieties. Opposite: Agapanthus lead the eye back to the magnolia hedge, which is kept trim and healthy through a regimen of annual pruning.*

garden and terrace; others were added later along the yard garden. A proposed brick screen in front of the garden gate was abandoned in favor of a low bamboo fence around a bed of three mature, coarse-leaf varieties of Japanese holly. The garden's defining element is the elevated, L-shaped pool in the southwest corner. Here, Richard Bull has shepherded Japanese koi to great size, and the first glimpse of them in such a confined pond produces a pleasant shock. The pool is part of a raised planter that extends beneath the west and south walls of the garden to provide room for climbing vines, perennials, bulbs, and shrubs.

The Norway maple, which had been kept to anchor the proposed

Splashing water cools the shady corner by the fish pond. Opposite: A sitting wall allows party guests to run their fingers through the water and feed the koi. The figures are native sculptures collected during the Bulls' residence in Africa. Left: The terraces off the house become favored spots during Washington's outdoor months.

sitting terrace and provide shade during the hot months, eventually died and was replaced with a daintier zelkova tree, whose smooth, high-spreading canopy of leaves provides the terrace with a more delicate level of shade. Beneath, a large terra-cotta pot contains a *Rhododendron* x 'Boule de neige' of splendid age and presence that blooms reliably and spectacularly in late spring. It anchors an array of other contained plants that turn the terrace into its own garden of scent, color, and whimsy—including various herbs for the kitchen, showy perennials (agapanthus and tall bearded iris), and a dwarf peach and a dwarf nectarine, both of which produce fruit. The bed between the terrace and the house contains a crape myrtle kept pollarded (and highly floriferous) so as not to interfere with a French-style awning that is unfurled in gentle showers or blazing sun.

By accident or design, two espaliered grape vines and an apricot plant along the wall of the terrace evoke the colonial and Federal kitchen gardens planted before and during the period when the house

haded in summer, protected in cooler months, the garden truly is used as an outdoor room. Right: As in some great country estates, the ornamental plants are put to work. Chives and peaches are among the herbs and fruit growing on the sitting terrace. The crape myrtle is pollarded to allow free movement of the awning. Opposite: The reflected heat of the terrace wall protects the blossoms of an espaliered apricot plant.

was built. Two common figs of similar pedigree in the raised bed between terrace and pool were transplanted in 1992 to the side garden to make way for camellias of the faintest pink. With its darker, more enclosed feel, its contrasting plant palette, and the drama of the magnolia hedge, the side garden is an entirely different landscape from the main, sunnier space.

The entrance planter contains at each end a large, coral bicolor azalea 'Hilda Niblett', whose foliage, like that of the rhododendron, provides year-round decoration. Between the azaleas a white-flowering Japanese anemone rises up in early fall and sustains ornament at season's end. Farther along, another raised bed is announced with splendid specimens of *Nandina domestica*, heavy with red fruit in November, next to a late-season azalea that blooms white.

The bed makes a right-angled turn into the house, where the garden becomes a woodland space of shady perennials, including astilbe, foam flower, and the magnificent *Arum italicum*, an Old World herb that in spring sends forth a Jack-in-the-pulpit–type flower with a bright orange berry. The plant disappears during the languid Washington summer and in autumn regrows its large, marbled arrow-shaped leaves, which remain robust throughout the winter. The garden's general hibernation, however, is short lived. Late winter- and spring-flowering bulbs have always been an important signal of garden rebirth. In the Bull garden spring brings forth a display of seven hundred minor bulbs—winter aconites, chionodoxa, *Iris reticulata, I. danfordii, I. tuberosa,* and crocus—which bloom and then yield to four hundred early-, mid-, and late-flowering tulips. Peter J. Schenk, Jr., the contract gardener, assures a long tulip season with six or so types, from the early-blooming Kaufmanniana forms to the late peony-flowered tulips. By planting the raised beds in bands, with the bloom sequence from back to front, he can plant abundantly and in a way that hides spent blooms.

With such bounty and diversity in every nook of their garden, the Bulls have produced a paradise for themselves and an inspiring example of how to transform a small city space into a garden of generosity and spirit.

HOPE AND FRIENDSHIP

There are many faces to the old-fashioned garden of Beulah Foster, but none more dramatic or beguiling than the walled garden off the dining room. Its high, cocooning walls, its expansiveness, and its distant ruined column evoke the peristyle gardens of ancient Rome. The Roman citizen would find some alien aspects—the entrance is not from within the house, and the solid whitewashed brick replaces the fluted columns of the classical atrium—but the garden has the same mystical ability to bring the outside in. On moonlit evenings, when the diffused lunar light reflects off the creamy brick and strategic night lighting is turned on, the space glows. The enchantment grows stronger for a few days in midspring, when the dogwoods and azaleas and wisteria bloom and the lightning bugs flicker. There is no other scene quite like it in Georgetown.

The Foster property was hewn from a picturesque, late Federal country house built about 1830 by William Robinson, a distinguished Georgetown lawyer. The property changed little during the nineteenth century—its high, sloping grounds allowed a fine view of the distant Potomac River—but twentieth-century progress has obliterated this view. Robinson's estate, called Mount Hope, had reached its high point by the late 1880s, when the grounds contained a large stable block and a greenhouse of extraordinary dimension, occupying far more land than the house. Such excesses were common in the new age of iron and glass. By century's end, however, another nineteenth-century fad was shaping the estate's new role as a gentlemen's tennis club. This incarnation held until the 1920s, when an eccentric but respected diplomat named Alexander Kirk purchased the property and set about revamping and enlarging the house and building broad formal boxwood terraces, including a lower terrace dominated by a swimming pool one hundred feet long and forty feet wide. He would ask unsuspecting guests if they would care to try his bathtub. This sybaritism paled, however, to the earthly delights of the last owner of the estate, Evalyn Walsh McLean, heiress to her father's gold mining and publishing empires. When she moved to Kirk's place in the early 1940s she brought with her the lavish style and the name of her former Northwest Washington mansion, Friendship.

The Georgetown Friendship, like its predecessor, was aptly named. Swimming parties turned the place into a veritable spa, the grounds embellished with heroic statues of gods and goddesses. Evening dinner parties were, in the words of one regular guest, "lavish and continuous" and attracted a steady stream of high government officials, diplomats, and movie stars, among them Noël Coward, Jeanette MacDonald, and Gary Cooper. Often, guests got to see McLean's most famous pieces of jewelry, including the Hope Diamond. During the

The "gaudy days" here are no more, replaced with a stillness and serenity in the grounds of what was once Georgetown's greatest social haunt. Opening page: Even from outside the old kitchen garden, the walls dominate and allow anchoring of ancient, well-trimmed wisteria. Detail: The duck fountain recalls the whimsy of days past. Opposite: Traditional in its symmetry and plant material, the high walled garden is unique, however, in its classical drama. A pair of old flowering dogwoods brighten the corners. The stark tracery of the distant ailanthus tree leads the eye skyward.

war, toward the end of her life, she extended the same largesse to wounded and homeless soldiers. She died in 1947, and with her a way of life never to be seen again. The dinner party continues as a key ingredient in Georgetown life but not on such a scale. No one brings circuses to the home, enlarges the house expressly for one party, or keeps three butlers—not even in Georgetown.

Shortly after the great hostess's death Beulah and William Chapman Foster bought one of four houses created from the mansion's center section and east wing. The old estate was no more. The grand garden terraces were gone, replaced with fashionable townhouses. The grand colonnaded ballroom, once likened to Aida's tomb, had been demolished to make way for more townhouses. Later, the Fosters bought the adjoining end section of the east wing, a warren of old servants quarters. It needed gutting and reworking but offered a doubling of living space and the amenity of the walled garden, originally the kitchen garden. The outdoor space was as dilapidated as the interior—weeds were shoulder high, rattlesnakes made their home there, and the walls were crumbling. This might have been a daunting task, but Bill Foster was one of life's doers. If he could reconstruct Europe after the destruction of World War II, as administrator of the Marshall Plan, he and his wife certainly could reclaim this garden.

Little has changed since the garden's transformation. Today, the formal dining room and its picture window allow dinner guests to absorb the walled garden's full drama. The view is simple and captivating. Two grand, ancient specimens of flowering dogwood, *Cornus florida*, stand in each far corner. The white backdrop plays to the dogwood's changing aspects: the blackness of its limbs after rain, the white blossoms in late April, the red berries and foliage in fall, the swelling ash gray buds in winter. Pink-flowering azaleas offer a splash of color in May, intensified by the purple-flowering wisteria, which yields to the deep red of neatly pruned climbing roses. The cross-axial brick path into the adjoining garden offers similar experiences but without the enclosing mass of the walls. Here, a red maple tree occupies the center space once inhabited by an old American holly that toppled after the

ground around it collapsed. In this garden Evalyn McLean had kept a pet bull gorilla in an iron cage. When it died, it was buried in the garden; eventually the grave caved in. Beulah Foster kept a straw monkey in the holly tree; at dinner parties she would feign surprise at seeing it and then suggest it was the ghost of the gorilla.

At the end of the garden is a path between old, billowing boxwood that winds mysteriously around the back of the kitchen garden to another garden space. Here stands the garden's other great element, a tree of heaven, *Ailanthus altissima,* whose age and size raise it above the lowly station of its species. It is the largest ailanthus in the precinct, perhaps in the city, and each season its sinewy black-gray trunk grows closer to the edges of its brick well, which is five feet across. In winter its thick winding boughs rise above the kitchen garden in a dark, almost grotesque fashion. The secrets of Evalyn McLean's Friendship are locked in its silent boughs. As Friendship's neighbor, the late Birne West, once put it, "The gaudy days are gone."

*T*he walled garden's sense of enclosure is lightened by white paint and a series of iron grilles that lend transparency and permit air circulation. Opposite: The dogwoods offer new ornament in the autumn, when the ruby red leaves drop to reveal ash gray, turban-shaped buds. Left: White-flowering trees and shrubs such as this crab apple reinforce the garden's restrained elegance. The column stops the axis through the walled garden. The ailanthus is surrounded by a brick well that allowed a raised path to the lawn terrace beyond.

CHERUBS IN THE BOXWOOD

The garden of one of Georgetown's preeminent hostesses is a great example of the old-style Colonial Revival gardens that are gradually being lost in Georgetown. It suggests a certain relaxed order, a place that can host a formal dinner party for twenty as easily as supper for two. It has softened through the years, as the boxwood and other broadleaf evergreens have billowed out, but its underlying form has changed little since it was designed in 1952.

How can a garden be both ceremonial and unreserved and remain so? The answer lies in the cultivated tastes of the owner, Polly Fritchey, and a landscaper whose name became synonymous with postwar Georgetown gardens—Perry Wheeler. A Harvard-trained landscape architect who spent most of his career in and around Washington, D.C., he remained true to his Georgian roots, bringing a southern sensibility to his designs, his plant palette, and his rapport with his clients and friends. Wheeler was a complex, cultivated man who viewed his work as an important part, but only a part, of a rich life of aestheticism. Keenly sensitive and quietly insistent, he shared his clients' sense of intellectual bounty and was as much at home in the opera house as in their gardens. His work was widely admired by the most important members of Washington society—he helped lay out the White House Rose Garden for his friend Mrs. Paul Mellon—and undoubtedly even greater fame and a wider

reputation could have been his if he had wished. But he was happiest when he found clients who would become lifelong friends and when he could make them a garden that reflected their tastes and needs.

The Fritchey garden, probably the best surviving example of Wheeler's work in Georgetown, is a case in point. Here, Wheeler was asked to transform a sloping, L-shaped, empty yard into a garden that would do justice to the Linthicum House, a large brick townhouse built around 1830 that extends deep into its north-south lot. Polly Fritchey and her late husband, Frank Wisner, a senior official in the Central Intelligence Agency, had the house extensively remodeled in the early 1950s, as did many other homeowners during this period of Georgetown's renaissance. Wheeler lobbied successfully for retaining the veranda on the garden side of the house, which today provides an exquisite transition between the house and the open garden, lends a southern character to both, and is an inviting and much-used garden balcony shielded from the morning sun.

While contemporaries such as Russell Page and Lanning Roper recorded their design rationales, Wheeler liked to keep things to himself; there is scant record of the cogitative forces that set a Wheeler garden in motion. A rare conceptual drawing of the Fritchey garden shows that his first idea for the sunken, classical terrace off the veranda was an elliptical space forty feet long. The garden's formal core came out

quite differently: it is half that length and rectangular, except for a sweeping arc on the east side facing the veranda. One can only guess why Wheeler changed his mind; perhaps the ellipse would not have provided enough space for the border plantings of broadleaf evergreens and flowering shrubs and trees, perhaps he wanted a rectilinear terrace to reflect the lines of the veranda, or perhaps the original terrace would have lacked the cosseting intimacy he achieved.

The remainder of the space contains straight-edged planted beds that meet at a brick path. Looking back across the formal terrace, one sees that the path steps up on axis to the far garden gate, which leads to the garage and a rowhouse mews outside. The path, in turn, is announced by robust, compact azalea hybrids in clay pots, which give way to edging plants of *Buxus sempervirens* 'Suffruticosa' and the tiny-leaf *Buxus microphylla.* It is a moment of subtle but captivating textural interplay that speaks to the unfolding depth of Wheeler's work. His gardens are architectural in the prevailing Colonial Revival–inspired style of his period, but even though he used plants as much for form as for horticultural beauty, he understood their individual worth. Boxwood was his material of choice—there are at least five types in the Fritchey garden, including a tree form espaliered around the end of the house. He worked closely with specialty boxwood growers, principally the renowned nurseryman Henry Hohman of Kingsville, Maryland, and developed sources for large, transplanted specimens from old estates. Much of the large boxwood in the Fritchey garden came from a Maryland inn that was being sold.

Wheeler's master stroke is on the north side between the back of the house and the high garage wall. Here, he kept his original idea of two interlocking circles, which he laid in pea gravel, edged in brick curbing, and brought together through a circle of brick set in the gravel. The shrub beds are pushed to the edges. The whimsical pattern of circles, the reflective quality of the gravel, and the sheer manipulation of void all together breathe a gaiety and openness into a space that easily could have become cluttered and claustrophobic. The gravel terraces were devised originally as a place for Polly Fritchey's four children to

$\mathcal{S}$oft clouds of boxwood and red brick make this a singularly American garden with touches of the Italian Renaissance. Opening page: The designer wanted a stage set that was both elegant and relaxed, especially in the evening. Detail: A pair of Venetian lanterns light the garden. Opposite, above: The lead cherub urn, collected by Polly Fritchey, fit perfectly into the classical plan. Opposite, below: Stone urns cap the piers of the garden gate. Left: The formal terrace reflects Perry Wheeler's typical subtle definitions. Its boxwood softens the edges without erasing them.

One of the last intact Perry Wheeler creations, the Fritchey garden speaks to an implicit faith in the longevity of the Georgetown garden. Opposite, far left: Henry Hohman's forty-year-old dwarf edging boxwood has yet to engulf the garden urn. Opposite: Wheeler's subtle interplay of broadleaf evergreens adds an enduring depth to the plant ornament. Left: Mixed tulips bring rare color to the garden and highlight the ingenious link between the brick circle in the gravel terrace and the tulip border.

play, but it soon became the preferred spot for dinner parties. The gate piers are capped with stone urns that, along with the cherub urn, two lead urns set in boxwood, and two Venetian lanterns in the gravel garden, provide important classical ornament to the whole composition. They were collected over the years by Polly Fritchey and placed with Wheeler's guidance.

The urns and lanterns, the strong lines of the terraces and paths, and the plant architecture suggest an Italian villa garden. However, the dense, fluid mounds of boxwood produce a scene that is singularly American. The garden is restrained and elegant but, in the best American sense, casual and supremely functional.

On showery late summer days, the urn cherubs dance in the changing light and the bittersweet aroma of old boxwood clings to the warm, moist air. A garden of such nuance cannot take shape on the back of an envelope. It is the fruit of the long friendship between designer and patron and their shared commitment to the classical style captured during Georgetown's postwar renaissance.

$\mathscr{A}$ CHAGALL GIFT

Like many Georgetowners who love their gardens, Evelyn Nef often starts the day with breakfast on the terrace. Unlike others, the garden before her contains a glittering mosaic by Marc Chagall. Often, garden lovers are also art lovers and vice versa, for both creative dimensions rely on an aesthetic appreciation of color, form, and composition. So the mosaic by one of this century's artistic geniuses would be enough in itself to lift Mrs. Nef's garden above the realm of landscape design. The mosaic, however, speaks not just to the powers of aestheticism but also to the deep friendship between Evelyn Nef and her late husband, John Nef, and the artist and his wife, Vava.

Ten feet high and seventeen feet wide, the work captures Chagall's renowned powers of diverse imagery and use of color and is the only one of its kind in a private garden in the Western hemisphere. Beyond its artistic

significance, however, Nef finds another, far more personal message in the piece: "It says Marc loved us."

As a young professor in Paris in the mid-1920s, John Nef scrimped to buy two of Chagall's early paintings. By the 1940s, as head of a University of Chicago doctoral program that required students to have expertise in several disciplines, including the humanities, he arranged lectures by leading composers, artists, and architects. Chagall, who accepted an invitation to lecture, found an intellectual soul mate in Nef, and the

two became friends. In 1964 John Nef married Evelyn Stefansson, an expert on polar regions and the widow of the noted Canadian-born explorer Vilhjalmur Stefansson, and she too was drawn into Chagall's circle. The Nefs and the Chagalls vacationed together each summer in the south of France. In 1968 during a brief visit to America the artist stayed at the Nefs' 1831 Georgetown home and said he would do something for the house. A few days later he announced abruptly that there would be nothing for the house. "The house is perfect as it is," he told his hosts. "I will do something for the garden—a mosaic."

Chagall returned to see his work unveiled on a balmy November evening in 1971. The predominant feature is the sun, in oranges and chartreuse, shining on two worlds: the temporal world of refugees arriving at the skyscrapers of New York, and Chagall's favored sphere of mythology. Pegasus is in ascent, Orpheus is strumming his lyre, apparently in serenade of the Three Graces. In the lower right-hand corner is found another of the artist's recurrent themes—two lovers in paradise.

Chagall made a point of not explaining his images. Possibly the mythological scenes are linked to America's guiding myth as a nation of immigrants. Perhaps the Graces are speaking to the sun (Brilliance), the immigrants' relief at journey's end (Joy), and the garden of the lovers (Bloom). Chagall cautioned against interpretation of his works, however. "Logic and illustration have no importance," he once said. "The visual effect of the composition is what is paramount." This approach, he argued, allows observers to attach their own symbolism to his images.

The mosaic is far bigger than Evelyn Nef had expected yet is perfectly proportioned for a garden that is essentially an outdoor room, approximately thirty feet square. Its enclosures of house, walls, and shade trees make it a naturally dark place from which the mosaic shines in its discreet but luminescent tones of gray, green, and blue.

Five years after the mosaic's completion, Evelyn Nef called on neighbor and friend James van Sweden and his business partner, Wolfgang Oehme, to rework the garden design. They kept a scheme that pushed plants to the edge of the garden and retained the "rug" of pea gravel. The designers' overriding concern was to minimize distractions from the mosaic; thus, they used uncharacteristically restrained plants in a similarly restrained design. The surfeit of shade also worked against the landscape architects' signature perennial style.

A large southern magnolia in the southeast corner next to the mosaic was retained and limbed up above the work. In the other corner a paperbark maple was planted. In the same bed, which extends back to the house, other small trees created screening—three Nelly Stevens hollies, with their glossy, thick foliage, and an *Aralia spinosa*, a clump-forming native tree whose drooping, compound leaves provide great ornament when viewed from the upper deck of the veranda off the house and whose bare, coarse stems decorate the winter landscape. In the opposite border stands a Korean dogwood, *Cornus kousa*. For understory shrubs in the garden's three borders the designers retained some dwarf azaleas and added *Mahonia bealei, Nandina domestica, Hamamelis mollis,* and *Skimmia japonica.* The shady, green woodland feel was fleshed out with more than twenty perennials, including hostas, lamium, epimedium, sweet woodruff, and lily-of-the-valley. A single climbing rose, *Rosa odorata,* basks in the one sunny spot, against a pillar on the veranda. It does not interfere with the gentle dominance of the mosaic or with its artistic beauty and message of friendship.

Chagall wanted his mosaic in a stucco wall, but the Fine Arts Commission insisted on Georgetown's traditional red brick. Painted a light, recessive gray, the wall is now hidden by English and Boston ivies. Opening page: Even in shade the work glows, and the artist's powers of color and imagery reverberate. Detail: Evelyn Nef once asked the artist about the lovers. "John and me?" she inquired. "If you wish," replied Chagall. "I wish." Left: Woody plants frame the artwork but do not compete with it.

$\mathcal{A}$ WALLED OASIS

The historic face of Georgetown hides more than gardens; it conceals the fact that the district is a place of constant, dynamic change. One of the best examples is the home of Nancy Gray and the late Gordon Gray. Their house and garden have grown and blossomed with Georgetown's resurgence in this century. Today, the hidden grounds of the distinctive yellow house unfurl in layers of varying proportions and moods. The surroundings of old hickories, maples, and willows belie the garden's proximity to Georgetown's bustling commercial core and through this guise add another dimension to the assemblage of stone, brick, and plants.

The gardens have been refined and enlarged over the years, but they still reflect the basic form and spirit of their 1930 incarnation, which must be credited to two women who were pioneers in their fields. Ruth Hanna McCormick, representative from Illinois and one of the first women members of Congress, purchased two adjoining late Federal clapboard rowhouses, both built in 1840, and joined them. A brick wing was added, and this was connected to a fourth building, which became the servants quarters. The available back garden space thus was doubled, and it doubled again with the acquisition of seven small parcels, known as tinker's lots, beyond.

The job of coordinating all these exterior spaces fell to McCormick's landscape architect, Rose Greely, who transformed the small

private gardens of Georgetown while her contemporary Beatrix Farrand designed her magnum opus at Dumbarton Oaks. Greely's designs were widely sought in pre–World War II Georgetown by discerning clients attuned to the garden preservation movement. Her garden at the Gray house is probably the best surviving example of her work.

The rear terrace was marked by a charming new brick pavilion with Georgian windows that evokes the period gardens of Washington and Jefferson's times. It stood in the southern corner, by a flight of stairs leading to the main terrace garden, which contained an octagonal fountain, boxwood-edged walks, and flowering shrubbery, all encased in Georgetown garden brickwork at its finest. Brick walls rose eight feet high, decorated with coursed bands, niches, gentle curves, and a series of piers, both high and small, each capped with carved wooden urns painted white. In the upper garden more brick walls of great ornament enclosed a sunken bowling green edged in flagstone. Bricks rose and curved to form Roman arches, and in one McCormick placed a bronze statue of a girl by the Italian sculptor Alfeo Faggi. Her face is frozen in sweet meditation, her hands are clasped as if in prayer, and her presence continues to have a soothing effect on the garden she inhabits. The upper garden is dominated by a nineteenth-century carriage house converted into a ballroom and theater for McCormick's other role as

*A*n artful assembly of land and buildings has created a large house and garden close to the busy heart of historic Georgetown. Opening page: A gate leads to the upper garden, the site of the ballroom and nearby greenhouse. Detail: The bronze statue by Alfeo Faggi brings a meditative calm to the space. Right: A shady corner becomes a perfect spring garden with dogwood, American holly, azaleas, and a carpet of Virginia bluebells. Opposite: The street front shows the successful union of two rowhouses and an addition.

Georgetown hostess. At some point a large greenhouse, forty feet long, was tucked in next to the carriage house, and it became as important to life here as the grand ballroom beside it.

When Gordon and Nancy Gray purchased the property in the late 1950s, the greenhouse had already been used to grow orchids. The new master, too, grew bewitched by the beauty of the plant and spent the last thirty years of his life growing them in his greenhouse. All the professional obligations of his long career in public service—he was a newspaper publisher, secretary of the army, president of the University of North Carolina, and chairman of the National Trust for Historic Preservation—were tempered each morning and evening by time spent in the greenhouse, where he would fuss over his favorite cattleyas, paphiopediums, and other favored genera. He became joint owner of an orchid nursery, Kensington Orchids, which today is one of the largest orchid growers on the East Coast.

The Grays made their own changes to the property, engaging landscape architect Perry Wheeler to rework garden areas and assist the Grays' architect with the addition of an airy sunroom. Wheeler draped the new conservatory and the existing pavilion in a diamond-patterned redwood trellis to support climbing plants such as a large-leaf cotoneaster and the vigorous pink climbing rose 'New Dawn'. He also balanced the parterre garden around the fountain, placed pink granite cobbles in the upper garden, and reworked the stairs to the pavilion terrace. The Grays later acquired more land beyond the upper garden, next to a site used first as a formal garden and later as a paddle tennis court and then a swimming pool. With the new land, brick walls were built to frame a garden for herbs, vegetables, and cut flowers.

As one might expect from a property having a succession of devoted gardeners, there are choice, old specimens of shrubs and trees, including southern and star magnolias, American and English hollies, crab apples, and common boxwood. Perhaps the most exceptional plant is a sourwood tree, *Oxydendron arboretum*, of astonishing size. The sourwood is part of the evolution of this remarkable hideaway. Time marches on, plants grow large, and others die and are replaced. But the bones of this garden, so artfully laid by Rose Greely and reset by Perry Wheeler, form a place of simple, classic beauty that abides amid the frenzy of the city.

A *succession of acquired parcels and different designers has helped the garden unfold as an urban oasis. Opposite: In the upper garden choice old saucer magnolias and woodland bulbs give a more relaxed feel. Left: The formal lower terrace was the creation of Rose Greely, a leading designer in Georgetown before World War II. A lawn terrace bounded in decorative brickwork tied the houses together and reflected the new grandeur of the assemblage. Perry Wheeler later brought balance to the fountain parterre.*

*T*he seamless passage between house and garden is through a tiled conservatory that leads, in turn, past walls clad in diamond trellising of redwood painted a flat gray. Right: The charming garden house serves as a library and is clad in a large-leaf cotoneaster. Opposite: The rose 'New Dawn' adorns the outbuilding's sunnier aspect.

Victorian Georgetown

ROMANTIC WILDERNESS

The poet Dylan Thomas tells us that death shall have no dominion. But death owns Oak Hill Cemetery: the dead buried here devised its quiet and pastoral contours; their grave markers give form to the landscape; and the presence of their earthly remains has kept the developers at bay. Death has dominion here, on the highest land in Georgetown, in a kingdom that speaks of sadness or peace or even joy but never with repugnance.

The understanding that the living can enjoy and use the domain of the dead brought about the American rural cemetery movement in the early to mid–nineteenth century. The idea of cemetery as park was the first unique American landscape style and led to the city parks movement, a decade after Oak Hill was created, with the construction of Central Park in New York City.

Oak Hill is not as famous as the movement's prototype at Mount Auburn along the banks of the Charles River near Boston, Greenwood in Brooklyn, or Laurel Hill near Philadelphia, but it is as deft a model of Romantic wilderness. As at Mount Auburn one enters through an imposing gateway to a level area marked by broad lawns, ornamental gardens, and a chapel. Beyond this plateau the great necropolis falls and rises along wooded hills and vales, until it ends at Rock Creek. More than eighteen thousand men, women, and children have been interred here since the first grave was dug in 1849. Some are modest in death—

simple worn tablets mark their remains—while others seek infinite recognition in large freestanding mausoleums or hillside crypts. Similarly, row on row of tall marble obelisks and columns attest to the High Victorian craving for monumental grave markers. Their verticality softens the broad horizontal lines of the hillsides, but not as much as Oak Hill's principal feature—its trees.

Disease and storm have taken their toll, but Oak Hill remains one of the last great woodlands in Washington to have survived the city's evolution, including the timber harvests of the Civil War. Many trees are judged to be between 180 and 250 years old, and a few oaks have lived for more than three centuries. The commonest species are white and red oak and the tulip poplar, although Oak Hill has its share of beeches and broadleaf and needle evergreens.

Below this canopy of American shade trees, a rich understory of small trees and shrubs brings nature to Oak Hill's hillside paths. In late April the cemetery glows with flowering dogwoods and redbud and stands of azaleas, a common combination in Washington, but here the breadth of the landscape enhances the plants' rustic powers. In autumn choice specimens of tree hydrangeas and sourwoods offer far-off tints of reds, pinks, and bronzes—an effect both somber and soothing.

The entrance lawns form the highest part of the land, a transition

*W*ith old city church graveyards full and insalubrious, nineteenth-century cemetery designers crafted pastoral land-scapes for the living and the dead on the outskirts of town. Opening page: A forest of obelisks reflects grand Victorian tastes. Detail: A family burial vault looks as if it took its design cue from Oak Hill's chapel. Right: Renwick's muscular Gothic chapel was constructed of gray gneiss and trimmed with a ruddy sandstone. Opposite: A flowering Japanese cherry cloaks an obelisk in white blossoms.

between the mortal world outside the gates and the immortal presence within. From every quarter the Gothic Revival chapel acts as a magnet on the eye. The majestic sandstone gates and the chapel were designed by architectural genius James Renwick at the age of thirty-one. By the time they were built, in 1850, he had already crafted Grace Church in New York City, and his Smithsonian Castle, so called because of its medieval revival style, was being built. Three years later Renwick was selected as the architect for New York's St. Patrick's Cathedral. At Oak Hill the spiritual link is achieved not through a cathedral's towering spires or lofty belfries that seek to join the firmament to the heavens, but through a chapel whose ancient and familiar Gothic form captures a sense of holiness in its human scale and architectural restraint and purity. The steeply pitched slate roof, Gothic arches, stained-glass windows, and a fabric of gray gneiss and brown sandstone give a subdued but decorative tone. It was built as a monument to unshakable faith and today offers the same solace as the day its oak doors were first opened.

Renwick later designed the original Corcoran Gallery (renamed the Renwick Gallery) near the White House, built for one of Washington's greatest philanthropists. William Wilson Corcoran, a banker and native son of Georgetown, also was the driving force behind Oak Hill Cemetery. Costs for purchasing the land and building its earthworks, the Renwick Chapel, the Italianate gatehouse, the gate and iron fence, and, of course, his own grand mausoleum amounted to $120,000. The land was sculpted with care to preserve its natural contours and ancient trees by Capt. George F. de la Roche, an engineer who is buried at Oak Hill. Andrew Jackson Downing, the father of the American rural cemetery movement, may have assisted him, although no surviving documents tell how or when.

Despite the misgivings of a Georgetown doctor who warned that the cemetery would bring down pestilence on the town, Oak Hill soon became popular both as a burial ground for prominent Washingtonians and as a park for its citizens. The sons of Abraham Lincoln and Jefferson Davis were both entombed here, and Lincoln wandered the

The entrance was placed at the cemetery's flattest and highest point, where visitors find the Italianate villa–style gatehouse, the Renwick chapel, and ornamental gardens. The garden here commemorates William Pinkney, a prominent nineteenth-century Episcopal bishop of Maryland, poet, and friend of William Corcoran. The cleric is buried at Oak Hill with his wife, Elizabeth. Grasses enliven the space in autumn and reinforce the cemetery's year-round interest to plant lovers.

same paths in the 1860s that the heavy-hearted Davis trod in the 1850s. A work by the great American sculptor Augustus Saint-Gaudens is found at Oak Hill but not, contrary to popular belief, his master-work—the cloaked figure at the grave of Henry Adams's wife, Marian Hooper Adams, which is at the small Rock Creek Cemetery, four miles northeast.

As the nineteenth century wore on, Georgetown crept north toward Oak Hill Cemetery. Industry flourished along the riverfront, with its quays and canal and railroad and warehouses. Oak Hill was a place to escape to on Sunday, a picture of swirling countryside whose open aspect and leafy canopy brought breezes and shade in the scorching summers.

The Victorians were preoccupied with death, for it was never far away. The Victorian philosophy of death reinforced the cemetery's dual role: redemption assured a heavenly afterlife, and the faithfully departed were never quite considered dead; rather, they slept. Grief was confined to the clan experiencing it, who in their emotional isolation glorified the idea of family and kinship. Thus, even in the graveyard the deaths of others could be set aside and the park enjoyed by the blithe living. Inevitably, however, the two functions clashed, and by the late 1870s vexed cemetery board members considered closing the grounds on Sundays to the general public because "cases of disorder are so frequent as to be much noted."

Today, Oak Hill Cemetery remains open to both the living and the dead (there are about forty interments a year). Rules continue to govern behavior, although twentieth-century sensibilities and the development of vast acreages of parks elsewhere mean visitors are generally reflective. The cemetery's Victorian image remains frozen, like the faces of the dead sculpted here and there.

Andrew Jackson Downing, reflecting on the appeal of the American rural cemetery, said that "the great attraction of these cemeteries is not in the fact that they are burial places . . . the attraction lies in the natural beauty of the sites, and in the tasteful and harmonious embellishment of these sites by art." Oak Hill, no doubt, fits his idyll.

The hills and vales display
specimen shrubs and trees at their
best. *Opposite, above: A sourwood
tree tints the landscape with
bronze autumn hues. Opposite,
below: A panicle hydrangea adds
its color to the fall palette. Left:
Obelisks and columns form a
vertical pattern against the broad
horizontal sweep of the land.*

MOON GATE BOW

Enlarging an existing house is a time-honored tradition in Georgetown. Even the earliest surviving houses were soon altered by owners in need of more living space. The architect's feast, however, invariably leads to the landscape designer's famine. Does enough open land remain for a garden? How does one join what space is left with the house and the new addition?

The owners of this 1849 Victorian end rowhouse were fortunate to find an inventive landscape architect to design a garden for the small L-shaped lot left after they substantially expanded the house in 1980. The result was a functional swimming pool garden at the end of the house and, on its reshaped side, a viewing garden reflecting the form and tranquillity of the Japanese contemplative garden. Linking the two gardens in a way that would not interfere with their key sense of isolation became the landscape's pièce de résistance. Gordon Riggle, the landscape architect, devised a Chinese moon gate of red brick as the perfect solution. It encloses the side garden without shutting it out, lends an air of inviting mystery from the garden gate, and sets the tone for the oriental garden beyond.

A moon gate is a rare sight in the Georgetown landscape, but the viewing garden itself is unique in another sense. The disparate building blocks of the garden—plants, water, earth, stone, and brick—coexist in perfect harmony. It is as if each has put one foot into the

realm of the other—the plants are architectural, the architecture is organic—and the result is a balance of sublime effect.

In the corporate world that landscape architects now inhabit, a place of button-down shirts and computer-generated drawings, Riggle might be considered rather eccentric. A keen daylily hybridizer, he is every bit at home in his own recreated turn-of-the-century cottage garden as over the drafting table. He stalks the high rows of sunflowers and hollyhocks in his wide-brimmed sombrero, looking like a country gardener. In truth, he is an old hand at crafting city gardens in Georgetown, where his adventurous spirit led him early on to experiment with paving patterns. His style, if it were to have a name, might be called Beyond Basket Weave. In his hands bricks are no longer rigid elements but plastic components of fluid compositions—divergent streams or winding ribbons, for example. This approach was perfect for the Japanese viewing garden, where he used groupings of vertical granite stones as the boulders around which a rushing dry stream of brick was devised.

Flecked, striated columns of granite chosen for their individual character and markings rise around clusters of smaller stones at strategic spots—to the right after stepping through the moon gate and in the far end of the space where a stone-bordered fountain creates the sound of trickling water. Around these monoliths brick pavers course

*A*dding on to a historic rowhouse became both a challenge and a new gardening opportunity. *Opening page: A brick moon gate entrance was the perfect solution. It frames an irresistible view to a garden where filtered light provides ever-changing moods. Detail: Lavender-pink azalea blossoms help brighten the garden in midspring. Right: The addition ate into the land, but its light-filled aspect, container plants, and easy access to the Japanese viewing garden establish its link to the landscape. Opposite: Striated rock and brick flow from the designer's sense of adventure and fantasy.*

in diverging arcs—one sweeps to the French doors of the house, the other to the foot of the planting bed. The stones were discovered in a stream bed in a colonial Maryland hamlet, Ellicott City, where they had been dumped early in this century as part of a primitive erosion-control scheme. They were no longer needed, and their proximity to a working cement quarry allowed access to them. Riggle, his client, and a work crew traveled to the site with a crane and flatbed truck. By the time they returned to Georgetown with their bounty, the sun was setting, and placement and orientation had to be swift but sure. That was left to Riggle, who allows field conditions and intuition to lead his eye as much as unbending blueprints. "I didn't number the stones," he recalls. "I simply remembered them as I pulled them out of the stream. If you try to intellectualize a design too much you're not going to do it any better than if you do it intuitively." They were hoisted into the garden from the adjoining alley "like Easter eggs," he says. The garden grade then was raised to the proper level, and the pavers were installed. The back wall of the viewing garden was another engineering feat. Rising ten feet in the alley behind, its garden face is much shorter. The finished grade of the garden is above that of the alley, and the soil was stepped against the wall to create a viewing embankment—a distinctly Japanese treatment of earth.

The central tree is a supreme specimen of *Photinia villosa*, introduced from the Orient in the 1860s. Its low, arching branches mirror the form of a Japanese maple of equal beauty by the moon gate, and its delicate clusters of creamy white flowers turn to fruit of great ornament in the fall. Riggle had first thought of putting a hornbeam in the spot and exposing its roots to resemble a large bonsai tree. The hornbeam, he decided, was not decorative enough and would cast too much shade. A Japanese black pine hovers around the fountain. Both the photinia and the maple have a high, lacy canopy that allows filtered light into the space. At the same time their leaves are backlighted by the sun. Each spring a Japanese gardener prunes the trees and other plants in his native style, exposing the beauty of the limbs. Night lighting reinforces the architectural elegance of the trees,

It is the little touches that make a garden special. Right: An unusual double-flowering or multi-bracteal dogwood adds interest and variety here. Opposite: Brick courses form a swirling river around the rocks, while the garden canopy is shaped by beautiful ornamental trees, including a photinia and Japanese maples.

provides focal points, and plays with the garden's sense of depth.

Flower color is restrained and the more potent when it occurs—in full spring the glow of deep-pink and bicolor azaleas and an unusual double-flowering *Cornus florida*. Annuals such as deep purple petunias and pink impatiens carry the moments of color into the season. Mostly, however, the ornament is on a deeper level: variegated liriope brightening and softening, ferns providing their delicate grace, and hostas offering up their beguiling leaf patterns.

The bottom edge of the moon gate forms a raised threshold, so that one must step over it to enter the viewing garden. This reinforces the separation from the pool garden. The opening's upper arch is six feet high, forcing all but the shortest user to duck a little to enter it, a gesture Riggle planned to suggest a bow, Japanese style, in homage to the nature beyond. It seems a fitting gesture in such a serene little garden.

$\mathcal{S}$ OUTHERN GOTHIC

No one could quite understand why Oatsie Leiter wanted the old, spooky house on the hill. It was wonderfully sited—high, distant, and mysterious—but its Gothic flourishes and air of decay made it the sort of property that caused the faithful to cross themselves and horses to roll their eyes and whinny. "It really was dilapidated. People thought I was stark, staring mad," she says. Restored and set in its relaxed southern garden, the house today is recognized as one of the Victorian jewels of Georgetown.

It was built in 1852 as a Venetian villa for engraver William Dougal and took on its Gothic form twenty-one years later. Nearby Wisconsin Avenue was a dusty trade route, and all around the house were pastures and woods, giving it the feel of the English countryside. This ambiance has been maintained in the one-acre grounds of the house but with a distinct southern slant. It is a garden that seeks not to compete with the yellow brick house, relying instead on sweeping lawns, specimen trees and shrubs, screens of evergreen hedges, and curtains of bamboo.

The Dixie heritage of its owner, now Oatsie Charles, is reflected in her plantings: two camellias were brought in cans from her native Alabama, and flowering dogwoods along with southern magnolias and American hollies abound. But the most essentially southern plant sits prominently close to the ornate front entrance. The southern pome-

granate, *Punica granatum*, is not supposed to grow as far north as Washington. Even if it survives the cold, the theory goes, the growing season is not long enough for the fruit of the beautiful carnation-like flowers to ripen. But here, in its sheltered southern aspect in the Charles garden, it grows well and blossoms. The top growth was killed outright one harsh winter. Others might have dug it up, but Charles bided her time, directed that no one plant over it, and eventually it regrew. The same sanguine approach has given the garden its character. Besides the camellias, now as tall as a person, several of the flowering dogwoods were transplanted from the owner's former Georgetown house, and the splendid hedge of Burford holly along the front perimeter was taken from the garden of her friend, the late newspaper columnist Joe Alsop.

The front steps to the house and grounds capture the essential dichotomy of the estate—both prominent and shrouded. The brick stairs rise sharply through the seven-foot embankment between street and grounds, veiled on one side by a leaning flowering dogwood and on the other by a mature, shady American holly.

Of all the plants on the property, however, one stands literally and figuratively above all others: the American elm on the southeast corner is the last of the mammoth old *Ulmus americana* that once graced R Street before the onslaught of Dutch elm disease. The Charles elm

*T*he house is a study in contrasts: prominent but shrouded, Italianate but mixed successfully with French and Gothic styles. Opening page: Spring brings a veil of lacy flowering dogwoods. Detail: The entrance porch reflects the grandeur of the house. Right: The southeast corner of the grounds is marked by a splendid old American elm whose lower bough has taken the form of a Gothic arch. Opposite: The elm's lower branches snake through the air.

is kept alive through a regimen of care aimed at suppressing the deadly disease, which is transmitted by the elm bark beetle. The tree is old and with age has relinquished the elm's characteristic upright vase shape in favor of a more oaklike spreading habit. The boughs are thick and low and meander horizontally like great serpents. One limb has done something rather odd and faintly mystical: it has grown into a near-perfect Gothic arch, and the similarity to the architecture of the house is eerie.

That a tree of such apparent vigor and power stands on the abyss is also strange and perhaps a little cruel. Charles has lost a magnificent old tulip tree to lightning and a flowering cherry of great size and presence to old age. The thought of losing the elm is too much. "When it goes, I go," she says, defiantly. Somehow, that is hard to believe. Charles is one of the enduring members of Georgetown society, as much a fixture as her house on the hill.

Instead of showy flower beds, the Charles garden relies on the subtle ornament of trees and shrubs and their relationship to the spaces around them. Right: Softened by wisteria vines, the rear porch is a favorite spot for relaxing in the late afternoon. Opposite: The entrance porch is both bulky and fluid and shows late Victorian carpentry at its most robust. Opposite, far right: Near life-size classical statues mark the transition between the sweeping lawns and shrub beds beyond.

$\mathscr{V}$ICTORIAN ROCKERY

Amie Block tells the story of two passers-by who once stopped to stare at the massive granite outcropping that dominates her terraced garden. "Look at that rock," said one. "I wonder how much they paid to have it put in," sniffed the other.

In place long before Amie and Huntington T. Block or anyone else arrived at the site, the boulder is perhaps the best surviving reminder of the picturesque cliffs settlers found at the upper reaches of the Potomac River. The area was dubbed the Rock of Dumbarton, after a similar promontory above the Firth of Clyde in Scotland. The boulder endures as a touchstone of the settlement of Georgetown.

The terraced garden owes its existence to the outcropping, which precluded any development on the site. When the Blocks bought the property the side yard was sloping, ill-defined, and poorly planted. The house, a grand Second Empire–style townhouse boasting a mansard roof and elaborate exterior ornament, was built as one of a pair in 1868 by Dr. Grafton Tyler, a prominent physician at Georgetown College (later Georgetown University) and a cousin of President John Tyler. As part of a modern reworking the main door of the house was shifted to the side, and the garden too was redesigned.

Today, the garden is bold enough to balance the house, yet it retains a secluded and intimate quality. The main boulder and its scat-tered smaller outcroppings recall a Victorian rockery, an image reinforced by the massed plantings of winter-flowering lavender and creamy white heaths.

The present garden, built in stages during the 1970s, was designed by John G. Shaffer, a landscape designer from Potomac, Maryland. Shaffer created a lower and an upper terrace connected by broad steps that follow the contours of the hillside. The retaining wall between the garden and the sidewalk was repaired and raised, and the path was paved and stepped in keeping with the landscape's clean lines and formality. A tiny rear plot of land was transformed into a viewing garden.

The garden's only original elements are the rock and an old southern magnolia at the top. The form and logic of the new garden relate to the design of the house through the strong architectural treatment of the terraces—their paving, retaining walls, iron railings, and garden furniture—and the fact that the steps to the lower terrace are on axis with the main door of the house.

This primary view is dominated by another southern magnolia, which anchors the far corner and reiterates the same mass of glossy-leaf texture of the magnolia in the garden's upper reaches. Six young hemlocks provide a feathery screen in front of the street, and this shady corner is underplanted with broadleaf evergreens—unvariegated

Aucuba japonica and *Mahonia bealei*—whose coarse texture is softened by the sheer scale of the magnolia foliage. A large Japanese holly in front of the border provides an accent of finely textured foliage. But even it looks coarse compared to the low hedge of the little-leaf box cultivar 'Kingsville Dwarf', which marks the edge of the terrace nearest the house. Its leaves are among the tiniest in the shrub world, and its glacierlike growth rate assures that the plant volume will remain unchanged.

The paving is crisp, square-cut flagstone edged by brick and a discreet, honey-colored retaining wall at the foot of the hillside. The broad granite steps up the hill gently curve around the boulder and through drifts of heaths. Heaths and heathers are difficult to establish as far south as Washington, and the sight of these healthy masses is a rare treat. Most of them are cultivars of *Erica carnea*—'Springwood White' and 'Springwood Pink'.

On the other side of the granite steps two Korean dogwoods balance the slope with their broad, horizontal habit. The raised patio at the top repeats the flagstone-and-brick flooring of the lower terrace, but here the emotional and physical remoteness from the street and house imposes an agreeable sense of seclusion. This is heightened by the placement of a stone bench next to the upper terrace's central feature: a limestone sculpture, *Strength,* by the Blocks' friend and Washington-based sculptor Pamela Soldwedel. A narrow border behind the bench is planted with Lenten rose, *Helleborus orientalis,* which brings down the scale and exemplifies the garden's unique aspect—its multi-seasonal interest. While other gardens struggle in winter, the Block garden comes into its own. The garden has its summer face: filtered shade and soothing greenery brightened by bedding plants of delicate hues. But in winter the lingering interplay of texture and the subtleties of winter flowers, fruit, and bark decoration create a more serious and sophisticated character. From Christmas to the first stirrings of spring the mahonia, hellebores, and heaths flower on until an ancient flowering quince—more a twiggy tree than a shrub—displays its clusters of dusky, deep pink blossoms on bare wood.

Besides the pieris, the back garden enjoys the canopy of a neighbor's southern magnolia and the visual focus of a handsome Chinese elm, *Ulmus parviflora,* grown old enough to display its attractive peeling bark. But its central feature is a decorative pool sited perpendicular to the house, which extends the space and mirrors *Quest,* another abstract carving by Soldwedel.

The rear garden stands in total and balancing contrast to the main garden. It is small, enclosed, dark, and secret, and the water brings a dynamic softness that contrasts with the stolid hardness of the rock. The main garden forces different virtues into play and strikes its own internal balance between hardscape and plantings and between its void and the house's mass. Its subtle references to Victorian landscapes—its iron furniture, its parklike quality, its rockery allusion, and its use of plants introduced from the Orient by the Victorians—speak softly of the life and times of the property's first owner.

Designed around an enormous boulder, the site recalls the days when part of Georgetown was known as the Rock of Dumbarton. Opening page: At the upper reaches of the terraced side garden, the elevation prevents the house from dominating while the layering of plants gives a pleasing sense of seclusion. Detail: The boulder anchors the garden and grants it an equal status with the grand house. Opposite, above: Heaths and quince frame the rock in late winter. Opposite, below: The sculpture Quest *in the rear viewing garden symbolizes Amie Block's vitality and, less directly, the garden boulder's immutable potency. Left: The brick landing gives the house entrance breathing space and establishes a conscious separation from the garden.*

149

MEADOW IN MINIATURE

In 1964 James van Sweden, a city planner who had worked in Holland for two years and had grown to love the ebullient natural gardens he had seen in the Netherlands and Germany, first encountered the work of Wolfgang Oehme, an expatriate German landscape architect whose residential landscapes in Baltimore were gaining attention. Oehme found the typical East Coast American landscape of lawns, broadleaf evergreens, and foundation plantings dull and lifeless. His work was born out of the naturalistic style of his homeland, where gardens were layered with perennials and small ornamental grasses and given structure by large grasses and specimen woody plants. Year-round form and texture became at least as important as the spring burst of color. For van Sweden, Oehme's style struck a chord: "It had a certain European feel to it. It reminded me of the gardens of [Dutch master landscapist] Mien Ruys."

Six years later van Sweden moved to an 1870 Victorian rowhouse on Georgetown's N Street. Within a year he was planning a complete makeover of the front and back gardens and called on Oehme to help. For two designers whose early careers separately had involved planning vast public spaces, the project was absurdly small. The front garden was a side show to the ten-second journey from sidewalk to front door. The back had tortuous dimensions: the lot was just seventeen feet wide and fifty-five feet long, and the sitting terrace off the house was only seven feet wide. Despite the constraints, the refurbished garden became a beautiful, functional space and assumed a significance beyond its tiny boundaries. The success of their first collaborative effort prompted the two men to form their own landscape architecture firm, Oehme, van Sweden & Associates, which has become one of the most influential and important landscape makers in modern America.

The practice has evolved over the years. Oehme's inventive plant palette has broadened even further, while van Sweden's designs place more emphasis on garden architecture. A firm that made its mark in private and public urban spaces now has commissions at large country estates, yet the underlying philosophy has changed little since van Sweden's own garden was built as the prototype. Their style is naturalistic but much more designed than the movements that inspired it—European naturalism and early twentieth-century American Prairie Style. It shares, though, their conscious rejection of the formality of lawns and clipped shrubs.

Van Sweden's concrete terrace was resurfaced in dressed flagstone and the retaining wall rebuilt in a buff fieldstone raked to look dry laid. Large-pane French doors were installed, and the finished landscape became a viewing garden from the kitchen table and from the terrace. The garden's winding path and the vertical and horizontal

layering of plants, however, create a sense of mystery that draws the visitor up the flagstone steps to the garden.

A sweetbay magnolia, *Magnolia virginiana*, sits at the front of the garden, replacing a *Styrax japonica* that succumbed to drought. Both trees are well suited to the town garden in their ornament and restrained scale. By placing them at the front of the garden, Oehme created a favored effect of a foreground screen through which the rest of the garden is glimpsed. This screening effect is reinforced by a seven-foot-high grass, *Miscanthus sinensis gracillimus*, placed a little farther back. A second specimen miscanthus is planted in the middle ground, by the path, and the ground between them is draped in smaller grasses: *Pennisetum alopecuroides*, with its nodding purplish flower heads, and the more upright *Calamagrostis acutiflora sticta*.

The journey is lengthened by distraction and digression until, at the garden's end, one finds a raised bed with a specimen Chinese witch hazel, *Hamamelis mollis* 'Brevipetala', and two Foster's hollies, *Ilex* x *attenuata* 'Fosteri', rising to meet a neighbor's Burford holly, *Ilex cornuta* 'Burfordii'. But the predominant plants at the bottom of the garden are a colossal pussy willow, *Salix caprea*, and, opposite, a tree of heaven, *Ailanthus altissima*, that has grown to vast proportion. The lower trunks and branches are smothered in English ivy. The vine's white flower globes appear in the autumn—a phenomenon occurring only on old vines—and are enlivened by honeybees before turning to black berries in the winter.

The herbaceous plantings in the garden, however, command the most attention, along with strategically placed stone globes by New York sculptor Grace Knowlton. The plant layering provides a purposeful manipulation of foreground, middle ground, and background that is both reinforced and distorted at night through strategic illuminations. The aim of hiding the edges of the garden is achieved by late spring, and by midsummer the garden has taken on its jungle feel that lasts well into fall. The sitting area and garden steps are given further interest with shrubs and perennials set in large clay and porcelain pots. In the summer after work van Sweden likes to hose down the steps and

terrace to bring a gloss to the hardscape (a Japanese touch) before sitting out with a glass of wine. The evaporating water cools the place and adds to the faintly tropical air of the garden.

Every landscape architect must master the third dimension—space. What helps set Oehme and van Sweden apart is their power over the fourth dimension—time. The emphasis on plants with strong seasonal cycles or multiseasonal interest creates a landscape that is constantly growing or receding, inexorably changing. Typically, van Sweden's winter garden is bony but not bare: wands of yellow mahonia blossoms arch above the evergreen clump bamboo *Fargesia nitida,* the two huge miscanthus are crowned with blanched flower heads above stiff golden stalks, and the magnolia branches are smooth and silvery. In spring, when all is cut back, drifts of tulips bring color and freshness to the reclaimed void. In summer the burgeoning grasses offer lush shades of green and the perennials provide sweeps of color, particularly a red-flowering *Hibiscus moscheutos,* common rose mallow. The long, sweet autumn is marked with the coloring of the magnolia and witch hazel leaves, the pleasant browning of the grasses, and the lingering blossoms of *Coreopsis verticillata* 'Moonbeam', flowering hostas, and a rare Japanese shrublike perennial, *Kirengeshoma palmata,* which produces furled yellow petals up to the first frost.

One might expect a garden so reliant on herbaceous perennials and grasses to be ephemeral. Yet for all its dynamic yearly life cycle, the garden has remained essentially unchanged for nearly twenty-five years. The tulips must be replaced, and in late winter a crew comes by to cut back the grasses, tidy up the perennials, and take an axe to the invasive rhizomes of the miscanthus. The whole garden is mulched and top fed, but it is then set up for the rest of the season. Hostas, ferns, and other perennials are watered in hot, dry spells. These tasks are not onerous.

In any case, for gardeners the allure of the Oehme and van Sweden garden is not the low maintenance but a landscape where outstanding plants are the principal components. This is a novel concept in modern landscape architecture, and it deserves to be savored.

By midsummer the garden is lush and mysterious with plants of exotic ornament. The feathery seed heads of the grass calamagrostis *capture the light, while behind the ferns the unusual and elegant shrublike perennial* Kirengeshoma palmata *prepares to flower.*

OPTICAL ILLUSIONS

Cynics might think that no beauty is left in the modern age, but the landscape aesthetic in Georgetown has never been as broad or deep as it is today. A generation ago city dwellers wanted a garden that would accommodate cocktail parties for their friends and a pool for themselves. Today, their needs and tastes are more sophisticated and worldly. Partying and swimming are still valid pursuits in the elegant American city garden, but they must be accommodated in a design framework that combines low maintenance with high drama.

The role of the garden has changed in other ways, with less emphasis on its social amenity and more on its duty as a private inner sanctum, especially in families with young children. Increasing land costs, particularly in Georgetown, have heightened the precious quality of the garden and the need to extract from it the utmost beauty and utility.

All these considerations were a concern in the mid-1980s, when Milton and Karen Schneiderman set about renovating their 1869 corner house and a small adjoining dwelling that was reworked as a pool house and servants quarters. They called on neighbor James van Sweden and his landscape architecture firm to design the garden.

On paper the design difficulties became immediately apparent. The reconfigured, expansive rooms within the house looked through balconies, French doors, and windows to a space of little depth. The landscape architects had to meet the clients' principal goals—a lawn and a new swimming pool—while creating unity between the disjointed, L-shaped lot and the unconnected lower area at the back of the pool house.

The solution, inspired by a San Francisco garden by the noted twentieth-century California landscape architect Thomas Church, makes use of eight-foot-square brick grids set on the diagonal. This diamond terrace, softened by the lawn on one side and the pool on the other, adds a second axis to the main garden that connects it to the pool house and what became its enchanting sunken garden.

As all successful small gardens do, this one relies heavily on detail, a high level of craftsmanship, and optical diversions and illusions. The broad diamonds of the terrace increase the distance between the house and the garden wall. Elaborate brick patterning within the terrace grids adds another level of detail. The brick diamonds are edged in creamy limestone stringers, and the plant beds pick up this theme with raised limestone edges milled with an incised bead.

Just as the ground plane is rich in such subtle embellishments, so is the garden's vertical face. In front of the existing garden wall, masons constructed brick arches that resemble niches framed in white, Doric half columns. This free classical ornament ties into the postmodern classical references in the refurbished house and is reinforced

At the former Schneiderman residence, Oehme, van Sweden & Associates was asked to craft a garden that would provide a private family retreat and bring design coherence to a difficult space. Opening page: Artful terrace patterning and bold plantings expand the garden view from the house. Detail: The front sidewalk border is crammed with multiseasonal plants, including tulips in the spring. Right: A lawn for the children was tucked out of the way of main views from the house. Opposite, above: The reverse angle across the terrace shows the dramatic clash of axes. Opposite, below: Flowering hostas suggest a woodland around the swimming pool. Sedum, coreopsis, and hypericum add color at the base of the bay window.

further in the new brick wall that screens the pool house. The sense of enclosure and privacy is bolstered by an arbor above the pool and an iron trellis atop the wall, which also provides support for robust flowering vines such as polygonum.

This level of detail was continued when the wall was extended to provide a screen in front of the pool house. The symmetry of the wall's arches and circles balances a space that otherwise would have been disrupted by the lopsided mass of the outbuilding. Despite the playful Chinese references, the garden's classic forms, the pool, and the high walls suggest a Roman pleasure garden.

Even with the elaborate detailing of the hardscape, Wolfgang Oehme's signature plantsmanship is strongly evident. The crisp lines of white limestone, which freshen and lighten the whole garden, anchor the playfulness of the perennials and grasses in the plant borders. Vertical plantings do the same for the walls—the weeping crab apple next to the garden gate, the espaliered pyracantha near the gas grill, and various plantings of the climbing honeysuckle *Lonicera periclymenum*. As with their other projects involving swimming pools, Oehme, van Sweden & Associates brought free-flowing perennials up to the edge of the water, including nandina shrubs underplanted with coarse-leaf *Ligularia dentata* 'Desdemona' and on the east side the even showier *Hibiscus moscheutos* placed next to the grass *Calamagrostis acutiflora stricta*. This juxtaposition of architecture and nature invariably proves exciting, not least because the pool becomes an abstraction of a natural lily pond.

The private side of this garden is balanced by a public face quite unlike any other in Georgetown. The owners instructed Oehme to soften the house, a challenge that no doubt delighted him. Limited by a space just four feet wide, Oehme devised a dynamic planting scheme that not only layers plants vertically but also stretches the lateral boundaries of so small a space. The effect is achieved through an extravagant mix of small trees, shrubs, perennials, and grasses. From tulips in April to the red berries of the photinia and nandina in December, the front border is not just a novel ornament to the house but also a public lesson in the rich rewards of bold groupings of multiseasonal plants.

*T*he garden has an effective
balance of perennials, grasses, and
fine woody plants, including a
Japanese maple of rare size and
form. Right: The high garden wall
is half hidden by vines, clipped
hollies, and espaliered plants.
Opposite: While most Georgetown
gardens shut down in high summer
and the owners flee the city heat,
this garden comes alive with
sunlovers such as rudbeckia at the
base of the maple and, behind, the
grass calamagrostis.

REFLECTIONS OF ROME

A boy growing up in the city needs room to let off steam. Nan Tucker McEvoy understood this and put off realizing her dreams of a beautiful private garden until her son had left the nest. After so many years of waiting, she might be forgiven for imposing an unorthodox test on the two dozen landscape architects who turned up in hope of a commission. Each was taken to the deck overlooking the rear yard, given a legal pad and pencil, and asked to sketch a conceptual design. Most were "not at all inventive." In frustration, McEvoy asked a respected local nurseryman if he knew any suitable candidates, especially for a classical design. He told her of David Campbell, a young landscape architect who was beginning to make a name for himself in town. Campbell, who aspired to create great gardens in the tradition of California's Thomas Church and England's Edwin Lutyens and Gertrude Jekyll, submitted to the pad and pencil test; he surveyed the scene, imagined what it might become, and moments later handed McEvoy a sketch showing a halo of small trees rising from the garden to deck level. Instant concept, instant commission. The garden that evolved is an artful blend of neoclassical Italian and groomed American rustic.

When Campbell began work, the land, which sloped badly in two directions, had no visual link to the highly crafted two-story deck designed and built as part of an earlier extension on the back of the house.

In preparation for the new garden McEvoy purchased from a neighbor land that extended the space back another thirty feet. Still, it remained a typically small nineteenth-century Georgetown rowhouse lot, measuring just thirty feet wide and fifty feet long.

A garden of masterful deception soon took form at the 1885 house. The reflecting pool was made deep enough to serve as a lap pool, and the fill from the pool was used to correct the slopes, build the raised beds at the edge for the trees, and allow for the underplanting of small woody plants, perennials, and spring bulbs. The wall would act as a backdrop for the pool and a cherished antique French statue and also screen the pool equipment. In all his gardens Campbell constantly sought to play with space and reality. Here, he forced the perspective of the pool—it is one foot narrower at the far end—to give the garden a greater sense of depth. Similarly the peripheral beds are squeezed in, as are the dozen Japanese tree lilacs, *Syringa reticulata,* that frame the garden.

The statue looks back to the house, along an axis that begins at the foot of the deck stairs. Here, a small lawn feathers into granite cobbles. A pair of plant beds are decorated with small-scale shrubs and perennials in careful colorful combinations. The beds curve to form the cheek wall of the grass steps to the sunken pool garden. The same juxtaposition of grass and stone serves as a unifying treatment throughout

the garden, including the blurred lines between stone and turf on the upper terrace and again at the foot of the back wall.

If the pool and its back wall speak to the classical idea of art and humankind, the raised beds, retained in walls of honey-colored stone, give nature its due. Important shrubs are repeated in both beds, but no attempt is made at rigid symmetry. Carefully orchestrated color was important to both landscape architect and client, so specimen viburnum, rhododendron, azaleas, and other choice shrubs anchor various groups of perennials, bulbs, and annuals in a cool color scheme of blues, whites, and delicate yellows.

In keeping with the sense of a small, polished woodland garden, foliage ornament became important. In late April, for example, the slender straplike leaves of the grape hyacinth are teased down the front of the wall. The lacy fronds of various ferns are buoyed by the sensuous forms of hosta leaves. Strategically placed rhododendron and azaleas offer leaf ornament year-round and then burst into creamy white

The garden blends the charm of an urbane woodland flower garden with the elegance of a classical reflecting pool. Opening page: Steps of grass and granite provide the link between the arched porch and the pool. Detail: Phlox divaricata and pansies are used to provide highlights of blue. Opposite: The pool and side beds are squeezed in at the bottom of the garden to give a greater sense of depth. The pedimented niche at the back of the pool appears to be one solid work in limestone. Like the adjoining wall, however, it is crafted from cedar. Left: wisteria vines appear to grow from the wooden side arch of the porch.

Clever combinations of perennials and annuals stop the garden from becoming too architectural and give moments of delight. Right: A long view of the right border shows the theory in practice. The leaves of the grape hyacinth are teased down the wall, while the yellow foliage of the emerging hosta picks up the soft yellows of pansies and tulips. Opposite, left: The step garden allows room for ornamental herbs set in front of a pink-flowering rhododendron. Opposite, right: Along with the crab apple, hundreds of tulips bloom in the front garden in April, always in one color and in the cool pastel tones of the rear garden.

and delicate pinks in May. In the curving beds by the small upper lawn, an ornamental herb garden sits at the foot of an autumn-flowering cherry. The curving bed opposite holds a specimen Exbury azalea and other shrubs underplanted with ferns and a white-flowering bleeding heart. These carefully crafted vignettes in the top beds and the side borders give a sense of perfect harmony and intimacy in a garden that otherwise might be overwhelmed by its architectural features.

Nan McEvoy designed the front garden herself before seeking help in her secret garden, and its success attests to her own design abilities. Built principally as a parking forecourt, it is paved in cobbled granite and ringed with the superior crab apple *Malus sieboldii* var. *zumi,* whose pink buds open white. Below them, the beds are edged with a double hedge, first of common boxwood and then Chinese boxwood, *Buxus Harlandii,* with its attractive coarser texture. In bloom or out, the front garden retains a soothing elegance and softness achieved through bold planting in a restrained plant palette.

Despite his emphasis on structural ornament in the garden, Campbell loved plants and knew how to use them. The tree lilacs, for example, were an ideal choice, for they have a more architectural form than the common lilac shrub and are freer from disease and pests. Their showy white blossoms last two weeks in June, encircling the garden like a cloud and raising the otherwise remote landscape up to the level of the deck.

The garden brought years of happiness to Nan McEvoy, although memories of its creation are tinged with sadness because of David Campbell's untimely death in 1984. Nan McEvoy has since moved back to the California base of her family's publishing company and sold the property. The garden endures, however, as a place where beauty and utility meld into a city paradise.

ALLUSIONS TO JAPAN

Georgetown's great building boom occurred between the Civil War and World War I, when the owners of Federal houses on large lots turned city blocks into land for Victorian rowhouses. Narrow brick dwellings offered comfortable quarters for federal government workers and, with houses typically just twenty feet wide, provided an intimate order to Georgetown's public face. The rear gardens were merely long, narrow yards—places to hang out the wash, put the outhouse, burn rubbish, and, if sunny enough, grow vegetables.

A place of Victorian utility, however, has become the modern landscaper's nightmare. When Barbara Woodward came to her 1905 rowhouse in 1988, her third Georgetown house, she inherited a garden that was just sixteen feet wide. Its narrowness was accentuated by its depth, eighty feet. Perry Wheeler, a postwar Georgetown landscape architect, had made a characteristically symmetrical and classical garden out of the space. A formal terrace next to the house led to two oval-shaped, pea-gravel landings, each flanked by Burford hollies and Exbury azaleas and edged by a clipped hedge in front of two stone statues of Pan. The whole was framed by two weeping Japanese cherries.

Woodward found the garden mildly amusing, but she knew that she would replace it. The landscape was too architectural for her taste,

and some of the plants were old and diseased. The garden seemed barren and cold in winter, the bottom third of the site was unused and overgrown, and besides the design had belonged to another generation. The new owner wanted a space that would flow more naturally from the house, soften the confines of her Victorian yard, and be better suited to informal dinner parties.

She turned to landscape architect James van Sweden, a longtime friend, fellow Georgetowner, and a man whose distinctive landscape approach was familiar. He had designed part of the garden at her second house before she moved there. Van Sweden's signature style, developed with his partner, Wolfgang Oehme, is a highly refined metaphor of the American prairie. Its palette of ornamental grasses, massed perennials, and ornamental woody plants is well suited to chasing away the confining boundaries of city gardens. At the Woodward garden, large grasses, shrubs, and ornamental trees would work with new design elements to break up the space into garden rooms, veil the stark edges, and provide a viewing garden from the house and sitting terrace that would change constantly through the seasons.

Van Sweden and Woodward were both fans of Japanese gardens and twice had traveled together to Japan to study them. Van Sweden wanted Japanese allusions in Woodward's garden but not Japanese

artifice, so he devised a winding, smooth stone path reminiscent of a stream. It begins at the new flagstone terrace by the house and ends at the bottom of the garden, flowing out into a pool-shaped form. A custom-built fountain of granite, topped with a pinwheel motif, sits at a strategic middle-ground focal point off the path, providing the sound and sight of water. The fountain is in a self-contained, sunken basin where recirculated water splashes freely and noisily onto small river stones collected from Woodward's farm in Appalachian Virginia. The fountain is detached physically from the path, but emotionally it is a part of it, an eddy in front of the remaining healthy weeping cherry. The path's expanse at the bottom of the garden provides the background hub, while the terrace off the house dominates the foreground.

Detail is key in a garden this small. The stone stream path originates within the flagstone terrace, resulting in a captivating tension between the clean, square-cut lines of the flagstone and the natural geometry of the stones. Symbolically, it is the point where the rigid architecture of the house yields to the idealized nature of the garden. The terrace is further softened by a series of large potted plants, including two orange-red lantanas whose berries turn a metallic blue at about the time the nearby porcelainberry vine and a Burford holly—both retained from the Wheeler design—provide their own ornament in late summer.

New tongue-and-groove fencing, lightly stained and capped with trellised panels, screens the neighbor's patio and enhances the Japanese tone through its clean lines. Against the fence the designers built a long cabinet in the same tongue-and-groove construction, capped with a thick countertop of flagstone. It is used as a buffet for al fresco dining, while the storage area below holds Woodward's clay pots, hand tools, and the other toys of the town gardener. Other hidden aspects of the garden include an irrigation system and a lighting design that accentuates the sculptural quality of specimen trees.

But it is the plants that give the garden its piquancy. The scale of the designers' characteristic plant massing is reduced because of the

Turn-of-the-century Georgetown rowhouses present trying dimensions for the garden maker. Opening page: The solution here was to mass plants to mask the perimeter without overpowering the landscape. The winding path, reminiscent of a dry stream, further obliterates the linearity of the space. Detail: Algae form decorative triangles on the stone fountain. Opposite, above: The porcelainberry begins its fall show. Opposite, below: Garden lighting gives an evening face to the landscape. Left: Twin Pans are set now amid the nodding wands of pennisetum.

In addition to hiding the edges, trees and shrubs are used to block a single view of the garden and add mystery from the house. The garden unfolds only when one walks the path. An elevated view displays the garden with its neighbors and reveals its unique introspective qualities. Smaller plants direct the eye to specific focal points. The yellow-flowering coreopsis, for example, coaxes a view from the front to the stone fountain.

smallness of the space, but it still gives bold form to the plants and allows the light to be sucked into the darkness of the bog perennial ligularia, for example, and deflected from the glaring blades of the ornamental grass pennisetum. Brilliant, dark, fine, coarse, upright, cascading—all these contrapuntal qualities march up and down, side by side, in a garden of underlying plasticity.

Flower color bounces around the space as the season progresses, and focal points change from one week to the next. Flowering bulbs carry the garden during its March and April dormancy, but in May the flowering perennials begin a show that lasts until October. Japanese iris, daylily, cranesbill, hosta, acanthus, liriope, and cimicifuga all take their turn on the stage until at season's end the drooping magenta flower heads of Japanese anemone arch over the delicate, pale lemon fog of 'Moonbeam' coreopsis.

As much plant material as possible has been retained from the old garden, including the one cherry, the Burford holly sheltering the terrace, the Exbury azaleas, evergreen azaleas, nandina, and the clump bamboo *Fargesia nitida*, which Woodward planted when she first moved to the house. But the new plant diversity has given her a far healthier garden and one far less reliant on pesticides. For all its Japanese touches, it is one overwhelmingly American in style and energy.

The two Pans have been relieved of guard duty and spend their retirement together near the back of the garden, facing the rear. Their white forms nevertheless provide background interest and, in their more relaxed pose, an appealing juxtaposition to the less-than-formal arched flower heads of pennisetum. Van Sweden has suggested that one of them be laid prone and sheathed in moss to effect a ruin, but Woodward is content to let them be as a reminder of her garden's journey.

Small in stature, this garden is nevertheless a symbol of the profound changes that are occurring in the modern American garden. A few of Oehme's plants may seem weedy to some, but they impart a different kind of beauty that, once learned, puts us closer to a natural world that we lost, somehow, along the way.

A Modern Village

$\mathscr{F}$ARRAND'S BOUNTIFUL HARVEST

The entrance gate to Dumbarton Oaks, Georgetown's most famous house and garden, is crowned with two gilded wheat sheaves, a motif that is repeated throughout the garden, along with the motto of its owners: "Quod Severis Metes" ("As ye sow, so shall ye reap"). The harvest on this elevated spot is bountiful and enduring. The gardens and grounds here embody the highest ideal of landscaping, the successful blending of human design and nature's beauty.

A progression of landscapes unfolds in a wide array of ornament, scale, and mood, each separate but related. In terraced gardens close to the brick Federal mansion, classical lines and decoration reinforce a sense of subdued formality. These lead to areas of informality, places of specimen shade trees and textural evergreens in gently curving beds, until finally the landscape's edges are blurred in areas of studied wilderness. The house was

refurbished and the gardens built during that golden period of American garden making—between the 1890s and the Great Depression. While other estates fell into the trap of being displays of wealth, Dumbarton Oaks became and remained a demonstration of exquisite taste.

This air of refinement and erudition is enhanced by the property's other roles. Owned by the Trustees of Harvard University since 1940, the house and its dependent buildings contain world-class collections of Byzantine and Pre-Columbian art and artifacts (in a 1963 wing de-

signed by Philip Johnson) as well as an antiquarian garden library of more than ten thousand volumes. The house was celebrated in Igor Stravinsky's "Dumbarton Oaks Concerto," commissioned in 1938 for the estate's owners, and was the site of a 1944 conference (in the music room) that led to the formation of the United Nations.

Robert Woods Bliss, a career diplomat, and Mildred Barnes Bliss, the heiress to a patent medicine fortune, had spent much of their early married life abroad. After World War I Robert Bliss returned to Washington to become a division chief in the State Department, a posting that convinced the Blisses they should find a place in the capital where they could build a garden, house their art, and eventually settle and retire. When they bought Dumbarton Oaks in 1920, it was a rather worn manor house from 1801 cloaked in an unsettling mantle of Victorian decoration. The grounds, built on part of Georgetown's original Rock of Dumbarton land grant, were similarly exhausted—cow paths and livestock sheds survived a nineteenth-century incarnation as a farm—but there was no denying that the property offered what the Blisses sought: a well-sited mansion in an expansive and pastoral setting in the city.

The Blisses were soon introduced to Beatrix Farrand, the niece of novelist Edith Wharton, who helped establish landscape architecture as a profession in America. In her calling as a garden maker Farrand

was, paradoxically, both an iconoclast and a staunch traditionalist: she rejected colorful and ephemeral gardens, preferring the subtle and lasting beauty, for example, of a sinewy old beech tree to the fleeting, garish flower schemes of bedding plants, but she held in perfect balance the tension between architecture and garden plantings and displayed great skill in designing with plants, the most difficult aspect of garden making. Mildred Bliss, with her own sophisticated view of plants and her knowledge of European gardens, was a kindred spirit. Together, they crafted the garden from the early 1920s to the mid-1940s.

Farrand regarded Dumbarton Oaks as her magnum opus, although she viewed it, like all her works, as a garden created for her client and not herself. Mildred Bliss made the final decisions—indeed, the Pebble Garden and the Ellipse, the two most famous features, were created after Farrand's retirement—but throughout their long relationship the mistress took care not to insist on landscape elements or ornament she knew her architect would oppose.

Beatrix Farrand had the ability to read vast expanses of land and design with comparable breadth. Right: Alongside Lover's Lane scilla, daffodils, and crocuses have naturalized to form a spring carpet. Opposite, above: More scilla pad the seats of the Lover's Lane Pool amphitheater. Opposite, below: On the Beech Terrace the beech's surface roots are interspersed with chionodoxa.

The degree of design detail and control by both women was phenomenal, even by the exacting standards of the day. This layering of detail on meticulously crafted space gives Dumbarton Oaks its sense of perfection—there are at least two dozen defined areas within the gardens and grounds. The scale and grandeur of the house are pleasantly understated by the fine texture of Georgetown's vernacular brick. The landscape complements the mansion on the south through broad informal lawns and on the north through formal terraced lawns on axis from the central door. The four terraces are connected by one of the garden's signature features: broad steps of brick risers and grass treads. The two lower lawns, once edged in boxwood and now framed by richly decorated walls of stone and brick, are squeezed in to force the perspective. They terminate at a large balcony overlooking a created woodland.

On the more relaxed south side the lawns sweep down and away from the house and are edged in ancient specimens of flowering shade trees and conifers of great age and beauty. Trees are perhaps the single most important element at Dumbarton Oaks: they lend grace to the lawns, form naturalistic backdrops, frame views, and provide shelter. Most of all, they imbue the garden with its vital sense of timelessness and define it as an American garden, despite its English and Italian allusions. Accordingly, Farrand took great care to build her gardens around existing choice trees and plant those that would perpetuate the sense of continuity. The katsura tree on the lawn, for example, was planted in the nineteenth century and is one of the oldest plants on the property.

The orangery on the east wing was built around 1810 and is one of the few relatively untouched original elements of the house. Outside, it is a masterful example of ordered late Georgian architecture. Inside in winter it is made lush with dozens of large, potted tropical plants, including hibiscus, lemon trees, the yesterday-today-and-tomorrow plant, *Brunfelsia australis,* whose purple flowers aging to white give it its name, and the climbing fig, *Ficus pumila,* planted around 1860, that today drapes the greenhouse's interior walls.

Two formal terraces lead from the orangery. The Green Garden offers a view of the splendid Italianate swimming pool. The adjoining

Classical sensibilities give way, slowly, to the romantic associations of Farrand's outlying wilderness. The succession from formal to naturalistic is often unexpected but never jarring. Opposite: Entering the hornbeam Ellipse is one of the great moments for new and frequent visitors alike. Shady and restful in summer, it takes on a somber, reflective quality on autumn afternoons. Left, above: The fall face of the herbaceous borders, however, is one of seasonal gaiety, with asters, salvia, and dahlias providing height within a multicolored rug of chrysanthemums. Left, below: The Fountain Terrace marks the eastern boundary of the formal gardens.

The informal spaces reveal some of Farrand's most inspired moments. Right: Brick paths converge at a striking Chinese quince tree outside the Rose Garden. The sunnier spot beyond enlivens the texture play among the brick, boxwood, and evergreen ground covers. Opposite, above: The mansion's south front is approached from the side. Opposite, below: The open north front, with its signature grass steps, reveals a far grander side to the house.

Beech Terrace becomes a viewing perch for Dumbarton Oaks's best-known garden feature, the Pebble Garden. Here a shallow pool lends a gloss to a mosaic of Mexican river stones. Baroque curves swirling from a wheat-sheaf design at one end are answered at the other by a fanciful but contained fountain. The garden, once a tennis court, is walled and framed by arbors thick with purple wisteria in April.

To the east the descent is no longer visual but physical through a series of terraces whose scale—with the exception of the small, parterred Urn Terrace—is reduced with each descent. Here, distanced from the house, one is prepared for the break with formality. Grandeur gives way to romantic woodland walks, where paths curve to places unseen and unknown, creating a sense of mystery and anticipation. One might turn right, through a cosseting tunnel of boxwood and conifers, or left, where the path turns and opens to an intimate, Roman-style amphitheater whose curved brick seating and a shallow, oval pool—Lover's Lane Pool—reinforce the garden's fey classicism.

In early spring embankments sparkle with naturalized crocuses and daffodils until, eventually, the line is restored with the straight edges of the cutting gardens, a sloping double herbaceous border, and the stepped path to the hornbeam Ellipse. Another signature feature, the double aerial hedge of clipped American hornbeam, *Carpinus caroliniana,* provides formality and openness in an area of the grounds otherwise hilly and increasingly pastoral in flavor.

The Ellipse is scaled perfectly, and its moods change with the time of day and the season. Sometimes the sinewy trunks are gray, sometimes green with algae, and sometimes, in the morning, black. To the southwest, nature is restored with a sloping embankment of forsythia planted in vast drifts. It is an area that once led to the adjoining twenty-seven acres of crafted parkland, in decline since it was given to the government in 1940.

Within Dumbarton Oaks, the vital energy and imagination of one of America's foremost landscape gardeners survives. The garden is open to the public most afternoons. But in many ways it remains a private garden, one of those rare earthly paradises that can still set the soul free.

The orangery is a splendid example of the elegant brick hothouses built in Maryland and Virginia during the early nineteenth century. Right: Tropical plants are brought in from surrounding terraces before November's first frost. The interior walls are smothered with a climbing fig planted around the time of the Civil War. Opposite: Benches of singular beauty were designed in close collaboration with Mildred Bliss and placed in strategic areas of rest and observation.

Farrand was wrong on one account: she believed a garden's life span to be about fifty years. Seventy years after it was begun, the garden at Dumbarton Oaks is maintained and replanted by a dozen dedicated gardeners. Right: The deodar cedar and weeping cherries behind the swimming pool fountain have replaced earlier, larger specimens that ran their course. Opposite: Superb nineteenth-century specimens of katsura and Japanese maple trees grace the edge of the south lawn. The maple has a spread of more than seventy feet.

FLORAL FANTASIA

The garden of Carolyn Agger Fortas looks as if someone had taken a Roman villa garden, filled it with all the soft romantic plants of an English cottage garden, and then washed the whole scene in the light yellows and blues of Malibu. This might sound unsettling, but the result is quite the reverse: the garden is a wonderland—bright, cheery, and filled with a childlike innocence. The mood is reinforced by the landscape's sunken nature. The garden is a large, open space but is enclosed agreeably—by the high, imposing brick house and its terraces and wings; by vegetation and tall walls on both sides; and by a towering hedge of clipped blue atlas cedar at the back. Light bounces off the yellow brick of the house and the blue of the swimming pool to pierce the darkest corners. Standing on the pool terrace, one has the sense of being in a classical amphitheater. All this drama and romance is no accident but careful orchestration by the owner and her gardeners and their shared dedication to intensive annual and perennial cultivation rarely seen today.

The house was built about 1945, but its classicism makes it appear at least a century older. The Fortases bought the house in 1965, the same year Abe Fortas was appointed to the Supreme Court. Carolyn Fortas, also an attorney, made her mark in Washington as an expert in tax law. As the affairs of Washington and the nation swirled about them, Abe Fortas found his calm as an amateur violinist (Sunday evenings were reserved for string quartet recitals in the music room); Carolyn Fortas found her solace in the garden.

The front of the house is softened by foundation shrubs, including an old, magnificent stand of *Pieris japonica*. The simple gravel driveway curves behind a clipped yew hedge that hides from public view a charming perennial border where spikes of lythrum shoot up like tiny purple rockets above lavender, rudbeckia, and achillea. A side bed is crammed with the extraordinary blossoms of the spider lily, *Cleome spinosa*, repeated in even greater profusion in the secluded rear garden.

The forecourt garden and the austere facade of the house only hint at the scale and gaiety of the private space behind the house. Here, a pair of elevated terraces—one roofed, the other open—sit at the ends of the wings of the house. A courtyard between them is paved in the same clean light gray slate; slate steps lead down to the pool terrace. The terraces connect the high, imposing house to the garden and contain their own moments of horticultural beauty, including perennials, roses, and even conifers in pots, as well as a pair of decorative iron plant stands where deep purple petunias highlight the yellow of the brick. The climbing rose 'Golden Showers' is kept pruned neatly against the railings of the stairs to the east terrace and, like the many

other roses in the garden, is treated in the spring with Epsom salts to
promote the low, bushy growth so suited to the town garden. Container plants abound on the house and pool terraces. Softening the
garden's imposing architecture, they include an impish array of miniature roses in reds, white, and yellows, and a herb garden of tarragon,
parsley, chives, and oregano.

The garden draws its symmetry from the balanced architecture of
the house and the central axis of the pool. On the west side a diagonal path of black river stones recedes slowly through the season as the
adjoining beds grow full and colorful. The creeping phlox, stokesia,
and dianthus yield to the profusion of phlox, roses, lythrum, rudbeckia, mallow, liatris, and achillea, and then the annuals take the
show to its climax—more cleome, cosmos, flowering tobacco, and
dahlias. The garden on the opposite side of the pool is a little shadier
and has a greater emphasis on spring color with such plants as creeping phlox, columbines, veronica, heuchera and lilies, but it too is full

The owner directs a type of intensive cottage gardening rarely seen in today's low-maintenance landscapes. Right: The heated potting shed houses a large collection of tender potted plants in winter. The flower border is itself warmed with generous plantings of gaillardia. Opposite: The swimming pool forms the heart of the garden. In winter it is covered with fiberglass and heated, adding to the garden's gentle microclimate.

of summer color. The whole landscape is in constant bloom from April to late October, aided by a microclimate that makes the plants think they are in coastal North Carolina. The reflective south face of the house and the warmth of the pool (covered and heated in winter) ward off the frost and keep fresh growth on the roses all winter long.

Even at the far, shady end of the garden, color is sustained with more perennials, roses, and flowering shrubs, including the reblooming lilac, *Syringa microphylla*. The view down the garden is bracketed by two buildings of splendid charm and scale: a potting shed and a garage of great character, with a low-pitched roof and a high brick chimney, clad in a climbing hydrangea. Connecting the two is the cedar hedge, an odd, dramatic treatment of a plant better known as a lawn specimen. In any other garden the hedge might seem jarring and excessive, but in Carolyn Fortas's wonderland it is just one more fantastic element.

As the season progresses, the stone path through the west border recedes with the growth of plants. Right: Flowering tobacco, phlox, and goldenrod offer scent and a preferred color scheme of white and yellow. Opposite: The whole show is anchored by the yellow garage, itself softened by a handsomely pruned climbing hydrangea.

ORGANIC HOUSE, ARCHITECTURAL GARDEN

Joe Alsop liked his vibrant corner of Georgetown. When he came to it as a young newspaperman in the 1930s, his block, one of the remaining enclaves of black Georgetown, contained a fine eighteenth-century house used as a mosque and various mom-and-pop enterprises, including a beauty salon and a funeral parlor. As Washington took on a new importance after World War II, so did a man who wrote about it. He needed a house that would provide comfortable shelter, a museum for his antiques, a library for his books, an office, and a place to entertain those in high office. An empty lot across the street beckoned.

Alsop designed and built his house and garden in 1949, and the rest, as they say, is histrionics. It is difficult to divine what offended the Georgetown old guard the most: the modern architecture, the mustard-yellow stucco, or the unmistakable lines of cinder block beneath the plaster. Alsop, ever perverse, delighted in the outrage that he had stirred in the capital.

Beyond its jarring fabric and form, however, the house on Dumbarton Street enjoys an architectural integrity that derives from its pursuit of function over ornament. Cinder block and casement windows are, simply, the physical embodiment of Alsop's ideas about space, proportion, and light; they reflect the need for the house to relate to its site and the desire for a thrifty New Englander to use the least costly materials available.

Alsop was no dirt-under-the-nails gardener, but he had an instinctive understanding of the spatial relationship between house and garden and the ornamental power of plants. He resolved the basic conflict between the inside and the outside by creating a house that was organic and a garden that was architectural. Moreover, he built the house around the garden. His office, his beloved dining room, his library—all embrace the landscape. In his parlor, which he called his garden room, the lines between inside and outside were further blurred. It included an indoor fountain, ivy crawling up the wall, and a towering philodendron that lent a distinctly tropical air. This was enhanced by his pet toucan, which lived in a gilded cage until the day it regurgitated a banana onto the head of a visiting dignitary and was replaced with two white doves.

Alsop reinforced this melding of architecture and landscape in 1961, when his marriage to the writer Susan Mary Patten (then widowed with two children) led to the construction of a second, east wing. This addition balanced the original west wing, brought more of the house into the garden, and turned the upper grassed terrace into a cloister garden. This arrangement is particularly effective at night, when one can see across the garden into the opposite wing and view dinner guests ambling through the house like ghosts. "It makes the house a living thing," says George Herrick, the second owner since

1975. "I don't think I really appreciated it until I lived here a few years."

Alsop's methodical approach to constructing his garden and rebuilding it in 1961 was done with the same thoughtfulness he applied to his other interests. On the brick terrace at the top of the garden—that crucial point where the house becomes the garden—he covered the patio with a large wooden arbor and draped it in wisteria. The deciduous vine shields the south face of the house from the high summer sun yet in its leafless state in winter allows solar heating. Here, dinner guests, among them President and Mrs. Kennedy, would sit for a cocktail.

The house in both back and front has been softened with climbing plants and foundation shrubs, and a visitor to the secret garden finds that the saffron walls have become backdrops to espaliered boxwood. Alsop clearly was taken by boxwood and its place in a larger garden scheme of year-round and soothing evergreen texture.

Unlike other Georgetowners who would move south in the winter and north in the summer, Alsop was tied to the place because of his responsibility for his twice-weekly columns. He enlivened the space by altering the ground plane, so that one steps down into the paths and terraces at the bottom of the garden. Along the central lawn this is accomplished with grass steps inspired by those at Dumbarton Oaks. The bottom of the garden opens up unexpectedly to the areas behind the wings of the house and is joined to the upper garden through a clever box-edged parterre shaped like a ribbed fan. It is interplanted today with lavender, rosemary, sage, and other herbs that reinforce the cloister garden symbolism.

In many ways Alsop's garden, with its tucked-away swimming pool and outdoor rooms for entertaining, reflects the prevailing landscape treatment of its day. But layered on top is a certain whimsy brought into focus by the trees. Alsop planted specimens in pairs—two fastigiate English oaks, two southern magnolias, two wisteria, two ornamental cherries, and so on. The effect is a sense of duality rather than symmetry.

George Herrick has taken over where Alsop left off. He has removed plants that have died or outgrown their space, added whimsical finials along the roof (in pairs, of course), and chosen plant material

Joe Alsop's modern house ruffled the feathers of architectural traditionalists, but it is an extremely functional home that drew many honored guests. Opening page: The rooms blend effortlessly into the garden through an open south-facing arbor whose wisteria offers shade in summer and sun in winter. Detail: Like other decorative touches, the cherubs come in pairs. Right: Alsop saw the garden every day from his office and wanted a landscape of soothing evergreen texture. He became a boxwood connoisseur.

with historic links to the region, including a pair of potted vitex. Two American hollies are planted by the entrance to the garden room, which was reworked masterfully by the second owner to bring even more light and delicacy to it.

The public facade, which Alsop softened with ivy, holly, nandina, and, up the spiral steps, spring- and fall-flowering clematis, has been further shrouded with two clipped hornbeam and four winter-flowering witch hazels clipped into standards. A hidden ground-floor moss garden set amid black igneous rock retains its Japanesque flavor. Herrick, a keen ornithologist, has added a bird house.

Alsop retired in 1974, moved to a traditional Georgetown house, and devoted his last years to writing about art history and collecting. He died in 1989. Susan Mary Alsop is herself an institution in Georgetown, where she still lives. The house that Joe built still raises eyebrows and, because of design restrictions, probably would not be allowed today. But those who know it love it. It brought a rapport between house and garden quite unlike any other in the parish.

The addition of a second wing allowed the house to embrace the stepped garden and create a private cloister where the newspaperman could fete his sources. Opposite: George Herrick has brought his own persona to the garden, adding rooftop finials. Left: Brick paving and boxwood form a garden more traditional than the house.

A lsop's beloved boxwood remains the core of the Herrick garden today. Right: A fan-shaped parterre of edging box spreads out to emphasize the broadening of the garden beyond the wings of the house. Lavender, rosemary, germander, and other herbs fill the gaps and add height to the feature. The abstract stone sculpture stops the eye at the end of the main garden axis. Opposite: The octagonal fountain gives visual focus to the upper terrace between the wings.

$\mathcal{M}$IRROR IMAGES

The home of Christopher and Deedy Ogden embodies the dichotomy of the Georgetown house and garden. Publicly, the house offers the elevated, elegant face of two wedded Italianate-style rowhouses. Behind this noble brick facade, however, the private side of the house reveals itself in light-filled rooms that lead effortlessly to a garden that is open and intimate, modern and timeless.

Phyllis Preston Lee and Robert Edmund Lee bought the property in 1955, when only its west half existed. Built in 1867 the Victorian townhouse—narrow, vertical, its bay front capped with a pediment—was like many found throughout Georgetown and all of Washington after the Civil War. One difference was to prove highly fortuitous: the house had an unusual side lot, and when the Lees concluded that they needed a bigger house, the open land gave them the option of larger quarters without leaving Georgetown.

They turned to Hugh Newell Jacobsen, a promising young architect, and his collaborating landscape architect, Lester Collins, an accomplished practitioner and teacher. Under the artful patronage of Phyllis Lee, a painter and keen gardener, their talents converged in 1961 to produce a house and garden whose whole is much greater than the sum of its parts. The project helped propel Jacobsen to national architectural prominence, made the house a local landmark, and persuaded the U.S. Commission of Fine Arts that contemporary architecture, if good enough, could work in Georgetown's historic district.

The transcendent value of the design is that the front garden and the hidden landscape behind the house became full partners in the composition. In most old city houses the garden is the space left over, but Jacobsen took the side lot and built a mirror image of the original house. The connecting section formed a new recessed entrance. The front windows were lengthened and lowered to reinforce the vertical rhythm of the house. The front garden was reworked to include an embankment of English ivy and, in front of the bays, low, clipped *Osmanthus heterophyllus*. Two sentinel *Pieris japonica* announced the second, broader flight of steps to the front door. This progression of restrained plantings distanced the house from the street and complemented the architectural show.

The vestibule doubled as an atrium dominated then and now by two mature container plants, a *Podocarpus macrophyllus* and a stunning *Camellia japonica* cultivar, 'The Rev. John Drayton', which flowers profusely all winter with carmine pink petals. A wall of glass behind both plants brought the garden flooding in. The Lees wanted an atrium to house tender patio plants in winter, as well as an ornamental lily pool and a garden that would require relatively little maintenance; hence, there is no lawn or fussy flowering plants.

Another factor that influenced the shape of the garden was the

T he doubling of the Italianate rowhouse created an architectural landmark in front and an architectural garden behind. Opening page: The right wing and connecting atrium were added to the 1867 house in 1961. The new windows, matte black and stongly vertical, hint at the modern treatment within. Detail: A waterside bench has become a favorite reading spot. Right: Emotionally, the atrium is part of the garden, with its mature winter-flowering camellia and, right, the podocarpus. Opposite: The linden shades and helps define the sitting terrace.

Lees' desire to keep an ancient weeping cherry with a spread of nearly fifteen feet. Collins devised a series of four terraces leading from the house and extending to the property line eighty feet away. The first was a dressed-flagstone patio that incorporated the Japanese cherry and wrapped around the protruding kitchen section of the old house. On the second terrace Collins placed the raised lily pool. Its design was deliberately bold and rectilinear, stretching thirty feet, three-fifths the width of the lot, and planted on both ends with specimen trees and shrubs. The terrace behind the pool featured more broadleaf evergreens and a crape myrtle; this tableau of texture garden behind still water was framed by a glossy, coarse hedge of clipped *Magnolia grandiflora.* Large shade trees from a neighboring estate continue to provide an illusion of great depth and a pleasing succession of plant scale.

The pool, stocked with ornamental fish and tropical and hardy water lilies, is two feet deep, large enough to sustain the water plants and fish but not so deep as to be classified as a swimming pool requiring filtration and a toddler-proof barrier fence. It remains the master stroke of the garden—the broad horizontal element that ties together the two wings of the house. The pool seems to reach up to the sky, grab the light, and pull it down past the reflected image of the texture garden and into the sitting terrace. The bold geometry of the pool, Collins remarked, seemed "the right thing to do. . . . If Jacobsen was going to double the house we had to have something very powerful to join the two parts together." Collins saw the garden as Jacobsen's synthesis of many garden influences: Japanese gardens, with the water, the fish, and the plantings in groups of three; Chinese gardens, with their yin and yang qualities; the Moghul gardens of Kashmir, with their broad, anchoring horizontal line; and, more subconsciously, the Mediterranean villa, in which one circulates freely between indoors and outdoors.

The plantings have changed with time, but the underlying structure is so strong that the garden continues to perform its intended mission. In the 1980s the Lees turned exclusively to hardy lilies. The cherry succumbed to its great age and was replaced with a now mature little-leaf linden that can be seen from the drawing room. The severe winters that

The large, rectangular lily pond ties together both wings of the house and acts as a mirror to the sculpted evergreen texture garden and cedar hedge on the levels above. The shrubs are sculpted in the Japanese manner.

ike the house, the garden draws its strength from bold and simple geometric forms. Right: The cantilevered steps keep the pool uncluttered and show the imaginative energy that shaped the garden. Opposite: The spectral quality of the fish and the constant metamorphosis of the lilies add layers of sensuousness and provide artistic inspiration to the owner.

ravaged Washington in the late 1970s forced a major replanting of the garden. The southern magnolias were replaced with the feathery, gray-green deodar cedar; it too is kept as a high clipped hedge. The texture garden terrace at its feet was replanted with many orientals, including three thread-leaf *Acer palmatum,* which turn crimson and orange in the fall, nandinas, mugo pines, and a Korean dogwood. The bed at the west end of the lily pond was replanted with a weeping cherry and a weeping hemlock; at the other end a Japanese black pine that survived the winters has assumed a sublime sculptural form behind a Chinese Chippendale bench. The house and garden side walls—designed as freestanding brick panels by Jacobsen—are clothed in various evergreen vines and espaliered shrubs, including photinia, English ivy, climbing hydrangea, and pyracantha. A young upright hemlock originally planted near the lily pond is now in the front garden, providing a tall, robust screen.

For the new owners the garden offers a place to relax in private, in casual dinners with friends, or in more formal gatherings. Christopher Ogden is a journalist and author, his wife an artist. She finds endless variety and inspiration for her work in the lily pond, where the water takes on a green luminescence in high summer, the lilies offer their own scent, color, and form, and the fish bring vitality to the garden. Deedy Ogden recalls the first time she stepped into the atrium: "I received a shock. The outside was inside. It just felt like I was home."

$\mathcal{P}$OTOMACK REVISITED

A decade ago, in an attempt to reclaim the forsaken Georgetown waterfront, architect Arthur Cotton Moore envisioned a landmark building that would link the red brick domesticity of Georgetown with the limestone monuments of Washington.

It would have shops and restaurants and boat docks to draw people to what had been an industrial wasteland. Office workers would fill one wing during the day. The night would belong to those fortunate enough to live in the luxury condominiums of the other wing. Among them, a very few would have penthouse apartments with exhilarating views of the Potomac River, where Georgetown was born nearly two and a half centuries ago.

Moore's vision in 1984 became Washington Harbour, a building complex that in recent years has claimed its own landmark status alongside its downriver neighbors: the Watergate and the John F. Kennedy Center for the Performing Arts. The architect's work has drawn mixed reviews for its bold synthesis of Modern and postmodern styles, but then the critics probably have not been inside this penthouse. Even the occupant of the White House does not have river views quite like this.

The view upriver is dominated by the graceful arches of Francis Scott Key Bridge. Opposite is the unspoiled beauty of the large, wooded Theodore Roosevelt Island. To the south the Watergate and Kennedy Center together proclaim the capital. Even these familiar structures, however, cannot erase the pastoral qualities of the Potomac as it runs through Washington. It is a view no landscape maker can or should ignore. In building and planting the balcony spaces around the penthouse, the challenge was to bring colorful garden elements to this home in the sky without trying to compete with nature's greater work all around.

The penthouse is set partially within one of Washington Harbour's round towers, which are domed and evocative of classical temples. The setting allows panoramic views through glass doors and windows but also shapes the sensuous circular geometry of both the living room and its balcony garden. A low wall topped with metal railings keeps people safely within the balcony without impeding the scenery. Built-in and free-standing planters offer midground color and interest without screening the horizon and provide a buffer for those afraid of heights. But the real value of the landscape architecture was in understanding that this was not just one balcony space but a series of spaces with different relationships to the home. The task fell to Guy Williams and his colleagues at DCA Landscape Architects.

The main balcony garden flows from the round living room. Like the rest of the landscape, it draws its presence from the detail and workmanship of the paving. Acknowledging the living room and its balcony

as the penthouse's most formal and ceremonial space, the designers selected a bright Indiana limestone that reiterates the light wood used in the interior, including the parquet floor. The unity is solidified with the paving design: four curving, concentric bands of pavers custom milled on a radius from the center of the room. This required an extraordinary degree of planning and control—not only to guarantee the arc of each course but also to allow for one-quarter-inch mortar joints between the pavers and their expanding circumference as they radiate from the living room wall to the railing.

Curving nine-foot planters, built around brick plinths for urns, are set into the railing wall—two to frame the view downriver and a second pair to direct the eye upriver and across to Theodore Roosevelt Island and the distant skyscrapers of Virginia. In late winter the planters are filled with pansies that step back in April for hundreds of tulips, typically in strong, warm tones of deep purple, orange, and apricot to give foreground presence. In May pelargonium and petunias take over. Elsewhere, free-standing planters contain broadleaf evergreens and small trees or masses of bicolored pansies in groupings of smaller pots.

The balcony arches back as it moves off the circular tower, sweeping past the French doors to the library, the dining room, and the bedroom of the owners' daughter. Here, the paving is of the warmer Tennessee crab orchard stone milled in squares and set on diagonal to broaden visually the balcony's four-foot width. Below, the view out is to Washington Harbour's esplanade and its focal point, a grand parterre and fountain.

Two lattice walls jut perpendicularly from this section of the balcony garden, and together they mark the private balcony space off the daughter's bedroom.

Again, planters soften the brick and stone and break up the lines of the balcony. A lead shell fountain topped with an arabesque relief and trompe l'oeil offers a vertical focal point between the two balcony gardens.

A third balcony space on the opposite side of the tower produced the biggest design challenge. Here, a small semienclosed terrace measures twelve feet by sixteen feet, but its awkward geometry, change of level,

The task here was to build a garden of beauty and enticement without detracting from some of the finest views in Washington. Opening page: In spring, tulips in warm tones bloom in the built-in planters. The John F. Kennedy Center for the Performing Arts dominates the downriver view, but unlike rivers through other capital cities, the Potomac retains its pastoral character. Detail: The garden chair recalls the wheat sheaf of Dumbarton Oaks. Opposite: Picture windows link the interior to the balcony. The ivy planter leads the eye to distant Theodore Roosevelt Island. Left: Paving is used to reinforce the balcony's subspaces. Here, Tennessee crab orchard stone announces the penthouse's private spaces.

The enclosed balcony terrace produces an entirely different feel. Right: The space's inward-looking character was reinforced with murals and trompe l'oeil. The green marble band suggests a rug. Opposite, left: The balcony room is protected from the sun and wind and is brightened by impatiens in contrasting shades of pink. Opposite, right: The curving balcony space looks back to the building's circular tower.

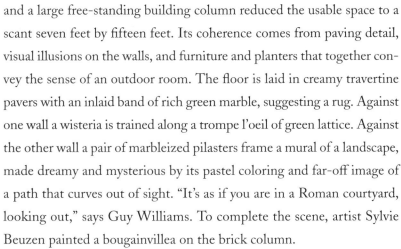

and a large free-standing building column reduced the usable space to a scant seven feet by fifteen feet. Its coherence comes from paving detail, visual illusions on the walls, and furniture and planters that together convey the sense of an outdoor room. The floor is laid in creamy travertine pavers with an inlaid band of rich green marble, suggesting a rug. Against one wall a wisteria is trained along a trompe l'oeil of green lattice. Against the other wall a pair of marbleized pilasters frame a mural of a landscape, made dreamy and mysterious by its pastel coloring and far-off image of a path that curves out of sight. "It's as if you are in a Roman courtyard, looking out," says Guy Williams. To complete the scene, artist Sylvie Beuzen painted a bougainvillea on the brick column.

People who live aloft need the bounty of the earth as much as other gardeners, perhaps more so. But making balcony gardens is difficult—drainage, weight constraints, and access are all real problems. In this case everything from soil to pavers was delivered using a distant elevator. Dry spots, wet spots, hot spots, and the near-incessant winds of the balcony garden bring a new dimension to plant maintenance and health.

The same might be said of all city gardening, even in the agreeable precincts of Georgetown. And yet the spirit of the gardener cannot be dampened. It is alive in the large old estates on the high ground, in the once-humble Victorian rowhouse gardens, and here, on the same stretch of river where it all began.

Washington Harbour caps the slow but steady renaissance of Georgetown and the river that first drew settlers here. Right: Where noxious industry once existed, waterfront bistros now attract tourists, residents, and workers alike. Opposite: The penthouse garden provides a spectacular aerial view of the complex's grand water parterre, the heart of this new urban mecca.

INDEX